Life is...

Common Ground

Life is...

Common Ground

Pat Perdue Davis

PUBLISHING Co.
Rutledge, Alabama

Life is... Common Ground
Pat Perdue Davis
AtL Publishing Co.
Copyright February 2018
ISBN- 978-1984929532

"To the outside world, we all grow old. But not to brothers and sisters. We know each other as we always were. We know each other's hearts. We share private family jokes. We remember family feuds and secrets, family griefs and joys. We live outside the touch of time."

- Clara Ortega

Foreword

I've always enjoyed creative writing. When I was a young woman, I intended to complete a hot romance novel and sell it for a lot of money. Life got in the way of my creavity. A few years ago, I started to dream of having a book for my grandchild and my precious little great nieces and nephews on both sides of the family. My grandmother, Annie Lou Folmar Perdue, wrote columns for the Luverne Journal. She had these columns made into a book. I have enjoyed them for years, and I really wanted to do something similar for my family. I am not the writer that Mamaw was. My writing bug grew due to Facebook and retirement. I have more time now than I have ever had. I just ran out of excuses.

You will find many reruns and stories that started on Facebook. You will probably locate plenty of errors and mistakes. I am old and sometimes accident prone. We tried to weed out repeats and typos, but please read as a friend and not as a critic. Perfection is an impossible goal and takes the fun out of most projects.

The title of the book came from Facebook posts and the fact that I end so many of my posts with Life is Good! I wasn't sure if I might not have problems with the copyright laws if I used that exact phrase. Also I found friends that I never expected to have on Facebook. People who enjoyed food, flowers, grandchildren, retirement, and/or family began to discover common ground because of my posts on Facebook. Once they replied and we started touching base on many issues, we were hooked. This has been fun, and I have laughed more than I've cried. Life is indeed Common Ground!

From Robert Guy Perdue
"Bob"

To my one and only sister Pat Perdue Davis:

My sister is unique. She is the first born, the only girl in a group of four. Early in her career, at maybe twelve, she was a producer, director. My earliest memory of this was when we put chairs on the coffee table to set up the stage coach. Us boys were always having to rescue the damsel in distress.

Some years later, I remember my sister keeping a diary. It was just everyday stuff that kids do, but it was important to her. I remember, once, finding her diary unlocked, so I read it, "Once."

I remember, my sister bringing home the prettiest, most popular girls in school. Then she simply locked her bedroom door.

I remember the day my sister took little brother Tom with her to school, "For Show and Tell." Why?

How much can one love one's sister? I remember the night before my sister was leaving home for the first time. It was almost like losing her.

It was the back injury, she received while working in nursing school that really drew me closer to my sister. She had always been there, producing, directing, and writing us into her life, teaching us boys to love each other.

Sometimes, my sister had a hard time with us boys. She is the only one of us in the whole big lot, who was able to stay married, "Once."

You know, as many books as my sister reads some of that knowledge had to come back out. She has been writing forever and decided to share a big piece of history.

This is Her Story. She has become known as the, "Life is Good, coffee drinking, plant lady," but most of all she is my sister.

January 13, 2018

Bob Perdue

From James Virgil Perdue
"Jim"

As most of you who will read this book will know, growing up in the fifties and sixties in the small south Alabama town of Luverne was like none other. Families were very close to each other, bound together by church, school, and neighborhoods. This was the way post World War families raised their baby boomer children in the South. Our family is no different.

In this book you will read about big family reunions, childhood Christmases and high school experiences burned into our memories. On the not-often-enough occasions when we do get together, we relive and re-love every memory. Pat was smart enough to record her memories in a journal that has helped frame this collection of stories. Pat and Billy Davis have made our family gatherings full of fun, fellowship, and of course, good food, a Perdue tradition. When we were children, my sister Pat Perdue was the thread that bound us tightly, and the thread has grown into a braided cord even stronger, through the blessings of experiences and trials of time, even as divorces, dementia and death affected our family. We are all in our sixties now. All still in relatively good health. We appreciate each other more now than ever, and enjoy that all are now sort of retired, enjoying grandchildren and living in God's grace period in life.

Thank you Pat for sharing our memories. Thank you for selecting the best ones and somehow editing the bad ones into something better than the truth.

Life is truly good. It is been made better by my big sister Pat Perdue Davis.

James Virgil Perdue

From Thomas William Perdue "Tom"

Pat, Bob, Jim, and then me, the baby. I am told that Pat wanted a little sister so badly that for quite a while after I was born, she would dress me as a girl and tell her friends that my name was Sue. That's right, Sue Perdue or Super Due. I tell Pat that anytime I mess something up real bad that it is her fault for confusing me at such a young age.

Pat and I have been closer than anyone else in my family. She would protect me from everyone, even today. I am so proud of my sister and my two brothers. When Mom became ill, and began the long process of death, Pat was in charge of everything. Never a question from anyone about Pat handling the finances. Well, you don't see that every day. Not a word about the bank account or the real property. We all trusted each other. Still do. As I get older and the body starts to disintegrate ....high blood pressure, irregular heartbeat, mini-stroke....the first phone call I make is to my sister, Pat. My head nurse.

A Little Beginning

As I recall, Mama and Daddy met in Birmingham. Mama thought that Daddy was following her when they got off the streetcar at the same stop. She looked over her shoulder and told him to get lost. He laughed and explained that he lived in a boarding house in her neighborhood. And I guess the rest is history.

Mama had been in the WAVES during WWII. Daddy had been a Merchant Marine. I don't know the order of things but I grew up hearing a story of Daddy having an 8x10 picture of Mama on the boat where he was assigned. They landed on an island and the native chief had never seen a blonde woman. He was after Daddy to let him have that picture to keep. The story goes that Daddy traded Mama's picture for a whole stalk of bananas. Mama often made cracks about keeping bananas in her kitchen.

Mama grew up in Birmingham. She was the oldest, but told me a story of losing an older sister, Beatrice, due to scarlet fever. As Mama grew older, she expounded on the story of her sister's death. She began to tell that her sister died in the bed with her. I am not sure if that is true, but it is sad. I think the family was in this order: Mary, James, Frances, Helen and Tommy. The family was very religious and pretty proper. The whole group was very church involved. The Birmingham Williamses were Baptists. In Luverne, Mama was very involved in the Methodist Church.

Daddy was the oldest child in his family. He, too, had lost an older sibling. I think I heard that it was another male child and was a

15

still-birth. Mamaw had Daddy in the same house on Third Street that she died in. The family was in this order: Jack, Guy, and Julia. I know that my granddad, Virgil Perdue, went to the Luverne Methodist Church. I don't remember that he went to any activity except the Sunday morning service. He always wore a neat suit and a hat. He was dapper and he was always straight and tall. Mamaw, Annie Lou Folmar Perdue, was short and a little bit plump in later life and was a jolly, loving person.

Mama and Daddy married in Birmingham (I think) on March 15, 1946. She wore a powder blue suit. Daddy mentioned it when I was a little girl and Mama laughed and said that he remembered it because it was the only dressy outfit she owned for years. I know that they lived with his parents on the farm in the beginning. I know that I was spoiled because I was the very first grandchild in the Perdue and in the Williams family. I was not the only grandchild for long. I was born February 23, 1947, and Bob was born April 18, 1949. Basically two years and two months apart.

Next we lived in Rutledge. I remember that we had some chickens in the back yard. I can remember getting chicken poop between my toes. I did not like it then and I do not like it now. I also remember having such a tiny rear end that I fell into the commode and had to be helped out. That is no longer an issue.

I had my first serious romance in Rutledge. I was madly in love with Bill Henry Welch. I loved his whole family, but he was the coolest. I thought that he was dipping snuff before he went to school. Turned out that it was in a snuff can, but it was a magical mixture of powdered chocolate and sugar that Miss Wynette made for us. So I had a cute Rutledge boyfriend and a bad habit at an early age.

My next solid memory was kindergarten in town in Luverne. It was held in the old community house which is near where the fire station is now. Ms. Audrey King and Ms. Hamilton were the teachers. I met some new friends and they remain my friends to this day. Stephen Coleman, Ben Williams, Drew Elliott, Mary Ann Helms, Annette Mitchell and a lot of other town kids. We used to walk on the sidewalk and walk up a hill to the park that is still the park in town. Pat Walker lived across the street and sometimes he joined us for play. There were some little boys in our school who were behavior problems. I remember sitting on the hill in the park in deep discussion with Stephen. We decided that these boys would end up in prison. The family moved and the boys moved with them. We never knew how these guys turned out.

I adjusted all right to kindergarten, but when I started Luverne Elementary School, that was another story. I hated the structure of real school. I went home from school early and often. Mama even tried getting some of the Perdue-Folmar employees to take me to school. I also remember her taking me to poor Dr. James Kendrick. I know that he had more important business than trying to talk Pat Perdue into willingly going to school. I don't think in the early 50s that medicating children had become a trend. Finally Miss Grace Fail just let me sit in her lap and somehow I finished first grade. I went on to the second grade. I can only guess that she was happy to see my backside as I left that class.

My elementary teachers were Fail, Davis, Mooney, Moody, Partridge and Hicks. I never really liked school, but I did like the social events. I enjoyed recess, play period and lunch. I remember delicious cafeteria food. At play period we arranged pine straw into rooms with doors and windows. It was flat like an architectural drawing, but our imaginations were vivid. We created families and relationships. There was very little structure to our play and that was the best part. I loved my friends. The best thing about a country school was that there was very little change in the profile of the class members. All six of my elementary teachers were experienced, and I lucked out and only got the teachers that everyone liked.

I don't remember much about the lower grades except having orange juice that was provided by some program… probably because the poorer children were not getting enough Vitamin C. We brought our own little cups from home, or we had to form a cup out of notebook paper. I also remember dried apricots that were often given out during recess. I liked them, but there were always lots of those orange suede looking fruits tossed on the playground.

I also remember the horrible series of shots that we got at school. The health department nurses came and gave us typhoid shots, polio shots, and maybe tetanus. We all hated the injections and someone would always faint or have a meltdown or throw up. I don't believe I ever had a dramatic event, but I dreaded those days.

I remember a project about the War Between the States in Ms. Partridge's class. I wrote the Civil War on my cover sheet and she did not like that. I saw it as the easy way out, but I still remember her criticism. I also remember a group of girls asking her what the "F" word was. She was shocked and immediately wanted to know who told us about that. It was Danny Glen Owens, of course. He was our bad boy. He was probably harmless, but all the girls were enthralled and terrified of him. He was known to chase down girls and kiss them. A fate worse than death.

I had serious problems with Ms. Hicks. She had the dance lessons. Bob Ausbon and I got tickled and stepped on each other's feet and we got a spanking with a paddle. Mama happened up at the very time that punishment occurred. There was hell to pay. Billy had to run to the classroom and he saw it as it unfolded . He rushed back to tell Ms. Audrey and spread the rumor throughout the 6th grade.

One more event was the formal Sixth Grade Banquet. Mama Mary was very much opposed to twelve year olds having dates and dressing like adults. I went with Bob Ausbon. We still giggled and danced together and most likely stepped on each others' toes.

Table of Contents

Life is...
Memories.

How It All Began...

And the beat goes on. Even more about the winter of 1967 at Bryce Hospital in Tuscaloosa.

My rotation at Bryce started right after the Christmas holidays, which I spent at home in Luverne. A couple of days prior to reporting to Tuscaloosa for psychiatric nursing rotation, a crowd of the LHS Class of '65 attended a New Year's Eve party at Billy Davis's parents' home on the Pike/Crenshaw County line on Highway 29. Billy's mother, Olivia Martin Davis, was an extraordinary hostess. Their house was beautiful with flickering candles, live floral arrangements, linen napkins and delicious food. And I started that night so mad at Billy Davis. He had told his friends that it was his party and he wanted me as his date. The guys were under strict instructions to leave me alone. I promise you that don't know me, I was no prize. I thought this was his solution for a certain date. He knew there was no way I would miss this gathering. I had been to several fall football games with his best friend, John Allen Butler. I mistakenly figured he would ask me to Billy's party. Truth be known, I was lonesome for all my high school classmates. Nursing School was a hard, serious journey. Many had fallen by the wayside. At times, I was hanging on by a thread.

I started the party a little ticked and cool to Billy. His mother had planned a scavenger hunt. We worked in teams and headed out with another couple to collect the items on our list. We drove to Glenwood and stopped at Martha McDougald's house. She and I went to her bedroom to hunt some random item. She has reminded me for about 50 years that as soon as we were out of earshot, I said, "That damn Billy Davis just had to be my date!" Most of you already know the rest of this story.

When we reported to Bryce Hospital a few days later, my roommate entered our dorm room to find me sobbing, as I had slung myself across that narrow twin bed. It is a pose that only a young Southern girl has perfected. Kathy Tucker asked me, "Are you that upset over this semester?" I sat up and blew my nose and said that it had nothing to do with nursing school. "I have fallen in love with a Luverne boy and there is nothing I can do about it."

23

She had the nerve to laugh. The first roses Billy bought me were sent to Miss Pat Perdue, Bryce Mental Hospital on Valentines Day 1967. The rest is history. Life is Good! Who knew!

He knows he's pretty cute for an old dude. Yesterday he made a special stop to buy my all time favorite sushi, Pink Lady. He packed it on ice to bring it home. He also stayed away from it and let me have the left overs for lunch today. He is well aware that old women love that romantical stuff. Don't think we have a perfect marriage. Oh, no! Those do not exist. We get mad and we get loud. And our secret is ......We get over it!

Stepping Into Adulthood

After a few sips of coffee, it hit me that I started to nursing school at UAB on the Tuesday after Labor Day in 1965. This means I actually remember the day that I stepped into adulthood. This was not an event that went smoothly. I was scared, homesick and country. Even 50 years ago, Birmingham was a big city and it was 150 miles outside my comfort zone. I appreciate the fact that Mama Mary did not allow me much room. Failure was not an option. I stayed. I learned. I grew up. This experience is a big reason that Life is Good today.

Birmingham Memories
1950s - 1960s

I would have been three years old in 1950. I started nursing school in 1965. I graduated, started work, and got married in 1968. My Birmingham memories are vivid. Going to Birmingham used to entail a long trip. Mama was so brave to drive it with three, occasionally four kids. She carried supplies, including an empty coffee can for us to pee in. No problem for the boys, but awful for me. Daddy seldom went with us to Birmingham. It was not unusual for Mama to get mad at him and take off for her family. Sometimes she went alone, but usually she dragged us with her. I always knew when something was going on. I was never certain if Mama's absence was a nice break for Daddy instead of a punishment. Back in those days, it never even crossed my mind that our parents would divorce. Tom usually stayed home with Daddy and spent most of his time with Mamaw and Duzzer (Virgil and Annie Lou Perdue, Daddy's parents). Tom never really got to know the Birmingham relatives.

Mama's folks always acted thrilled to see us. For a long time, I was the only girl cousin. I loved my aunts and uncles. I loved my cousins. We were a loud and rowdy bunch. Tommie Sue and James lived next door to Grandmother. I knew them best. For a while Mama's younger sister, Helen, lived right down the street. Her other sister lived several miles to the west of Grandmother.

Tommy, the baby in the family, eventually ended up in the Gulf Coast. He worked at the military bases in the area, but he was not in the service.

I really do think that all the people in Mama's family - the Williamses - were smart. More later about the aunts and uncles.

****

Mama's sister Frances was married to Jack Hand. Uncle Jack was an engineer at WBRC television station in Birmingham. WBRC came on the air on July 4, 1949. As with all my aunts and uncles, I thought that Jack ran that television station. When we went to Birmingham, we were often on the local broadcast children's show.

One of the first things I remember is visiting with Jack and Frances when they lived in the little apartment in Grandmother Williams' house. The first time I remember watching television was in their living room. This was a big deal to me. I don't think there were any television sets in Crenshaw County. Or maybe it all came into being at about the same time. WSFA came on the air on Christmas Day in 1954. Gunsmoke came on the air in 1955. I would have been eight years old then. I remember cuddling up on the couch and watching Matt Dillon, Miss Kitty, Doc Adams, and Festus. It was a fantastic western. It continued to be broadcast until 1975.

Another door that Jack Hand opened for me when I was older was the telethon in Birmingham that coincided with the Jerry Lewis Telethon nationally. He got me a special back stage pass. Every year I got to meet celebrities, in person. I kept an autograph book and followed these stars through the years.

When Jack and Frances moved across town, I often spent the night with them. I remember being shocked that my cousins talked back to their mother. Frances looked like my Mama and had many similar characteristics. I was so afraid of my own Mama and she put up with absolutely no smart mouth.

Billy Hand was the youngest child in that family. He was the first student I ever personally knew who had the term "Gifted" applied to him. He went to a special smart school. When I was in nursing school, I occasionally picked him up at the school. He was always glad to see me and I kept him from having to ride the city bus.

****

I remember being fascinated with the Birmingham streetcars. I remember clearly the sparks that flew from the overhead lines. And the clickety clack noise of the railings. I was six or so when the city operated streetcars were eliminated. The buses were interesting, but not nearly as much as the streetcars.

Life is ... Common Ground

I adored going downtown to the department stores and riding the escalators. I had such good relatives. Tommie Sue would take me and her boys downtown and wait patiently while I rode up and down on the escalators time after time. The city seemed so much more exciting than the country. I constantly wanted to be going and doing when I visited with the Williamses. Those days were a different time and it seemed that very few parents worried about anyone bothering their children. Grandmother lived down the hill from Birmingham Southern College and a few blocks away from Legion Field. There was constantly some activity going on. Also the whole family attended a very large Baptist Church.

I remember after church Grandmother would send Tommy to buy fresh rolls for lunch. We went to a small local bakery. Tommy would treat me to a cream horn. I remember that they cost a nickel. I would gobble it down on the way to lunch at Grandmother's house so that I didn't have to share. I still love that treat and every single time I eat them, I think of my Uncle Tommy.

Another thing I remember about the Baptist Church was that certain men in the congregation would shout loudly "Amen!" I think this happened when the preacher made a strong point which they agreed with. The first time that happened, it frightened me and I nearly bolted out of my seat. Luverne Methodist was a calm, quiet church. I had never heard anyone get excited in that church.

****

I remember that Tommy worked at a big grocery store as a young man. I think he stocked shelves. He may have gotten this job through Helen's husband, Jack Bailey. I think that pop beads came along with cases of coffee or some grocery staple. Tommy saved these beads. He had given plenty to his love, Amelia Agricola, his fiance. When I came to visit, he gave me a pile of my own pop beads. Such a special thrill!

****

Bear Bryant & the Sunbeam

Once when I was just beginning in nursing school, probably 1965 or maybe '66, Mama came up and spent the weekend with her mother. Someone from Luverne had given Mama some free tickets to the Bama game that weekend at Legion Field. My grandmother's home was only a few blocks from the football stadium. Easily walking distance for us. The weather on football Saturday was cloudy and overcast. I hoped that it wouldn't rain because we would have to walk back to Grandmother's in the wet.

At this time in my life, I was not a big fan of Auburn or Alabama. UAB was not considered part of the University in Tuscaloosa or at least not enough for me to get student prices on football tickets. Mama and I were both football fans and were ready to enjoy our day.

We had arrived fairly early. The Bama team was on the field

warming up and tossing balls around. We looked to the entrance to the field and a few coaches begin to arrive. At the very moment that Bear stepped onto the field, a large sunbeam appeared. The light fell right on his hounds tooth hat. The Bama fans erupted into a true roar. My arms were covered in goose bumps and the hair at the back of my neck was standing on end. This moment has stuck in my mind for years. Every person seated in the stadium was aware and focused on Bear Bryant. That day he was truly larger than life.

****

Yesterday I was out and about with a long to-do list. Several friends expressed an interest in more stories about my days of nursing school at Bryce Hospital.

That picture of an old space heater stirred so many memories. Our rotation in Tuscaloosa was definitely like residing on a movie set. My individual assignment was on a unit with adult, male patients. We were told that at least half of our patients had committed murder and were found guilty by reason of insanity. At first we were all understandably nervous, but we soon realized that these patients were just people.
One cold morning when a group of us walked to our duty station, we were told that there was a razor blade missing after patient shower time. I have chill bumps as I write about this. Remember we were nearly all college age girls and I had not reached my fighting weight at this point. We were each given a key to the entry door and we were to attach that key to our underwear with a huge safety pin. Personally I was a wreck when we entered the ward that morning. To make the day even more miserable, it was cold. I could see my shaky breath when I exhaled.
Our assignment was to interact with the patients. I joined a group around a huge, glowing space heater. We chatted about the weather and the bacon we had been served at breakfast, pretty much the same Southern small talk we grew up with. Across the room I spied this giant of a fellow that I had met earlier in the week. He

grew up in Opp and he knew I was from Luverne, a neighboring town. He walked directly to me and he held his gigantic hands behind his back. When he stopped in front of me, he jerked his hands about 3 inches from me and said, "Here!". My mind saw a shiny razorblade as it plunged into my chest. I jumped back into the grate of the space heater and melted my thick winter stockings. No pants allowed for students. Then I jumped forward into this mental patient's arms. The gentle giant had brought me a shiny, red apple from his kitchen work assignment. We made eye contact. He laughed. I laughed. All the patients and my nursing school buds huddled around the heater laughed. My legs weren't seriously burned. My pride was bruised or maybe singed. Later the lost razor blade was located on the edge of a sink where it was left following someone's morning shave. I learned more lessons at Bryce than I did from any psychology textbooks.

****

Another withdrawal from my memory bank about my nursing rotation at Bryce Mental Hospital in 1967.
I recall the onsite cafeteria for students. I don't think our days started as early as they would have back in Birmingham. We also got to wear street clothes, but I remind you again.....no pants. Seems unbelievable now, but oh, so true. Our first morning at Bryce was cold, cloudy, and confusing. We were just learning the ropes at our new, temporary home.
I love breakfast, but when we entered the student cafeteria for the first time, I was stunned to see mental health patients manning the food line. Not exactly Morrison's. And your question is most likely "How did you know the workers were patients?" Whoever in later years did the casting for One Flew Over the Cuckoo's Nest and Sling Blade were spot on. The character who immediately comes to mind was a thin, delicate dishwater blonde, who had her long hair in braids. She wore a leather strap around her forehead with a huge turkey feather in the back. She was Pocahontas. She served the scrambled eggs and did so with the demeanor and decorum

of a member of the British Royal Guard. No hint of a smile or acknowledgement of our presence. Our food was delicious. The coffee was strong and hot. We sat at long wooden tables and pondered our new assignments. This was a unique and interesting learning experience. Every journey does begin with the first step. Mine started with a Southern breakfast served by an Indian maiden.

****

Glad I made a few notes while it was cold and dark last week. The weather has warmed up and some of my vivid Bryce memories have faded, but the notes are serving their purpose.

While participating in our psychiatric nursing rotation, we were taught to make Interpersonal Relationship Notes. We submitted the notes to our instructors and the IPR notes were part of our grades. We wrote down what the patients said, what we said, what we thought this meant, and how it related to the mental illness of the particular patient. It was primarily busy work or it felt that way to me. IPR notes were a requirement and we did them.

I remember spending a lot of my time on the unit playing cards with a certain table of young men. It felt like home. They also supplied lots of material for my IPR notes. The guys encouraged me to join in their card game. When I asked one of them to shuffle the cards for me, I took a lot of ribbing from the group. I clearly remember one of them saying, "We are locked up in here. You are walking around outside and can't shuffle your own cards. Aren't you about 20 years old?" He made his point. They taught me to shuffle my own cards. They also taught me a whole lot more about life. Most of them had been in trouble at home, then in jail and soon had been stuck in a holding pattern in a mental health facility. I had plenty to write about....abuse, neglect, too much anger, violence, and not near enough love. And yet these boys seemed normal, funny, and so average. We laughed and talked and watched the world go by.

One day one of the guys said, "Hold up on the cards and look over your shoulder. You fixing to see something" Two old men were meeting each other in the middle of the big room. Someone was playing soft classical music on the radio. The men slipped into each other's arms and proceeded to dance a formal waltz. When the dance was done, they properly bowed to each other and went in opposite directions.

The card players smiled and the guy who had told me to watch, asked, "Bet you never seen that before." I told him I hadn't. He laughed and told me he was hoping to go home and was holding out to dance with a pretty girl one day. I told him I hoped he got that chance.

Now friends, this happened 50 years ago this winter. I do think the world has changed a lot. Lessons are taught and learned in some strange and interesting locations.

****

I think Mama's brother, James Williams, was an engineer with TCI.

I remember Birmingham when the black dust was everywhere. Grandmother had to take a damp rag and wipe the black residue from the steel mills from her clothes line. I loved helping her wash because she had an old washer that required running clothes through the ringer. It was somewhat dangerous, so I loved it. We would drag the washer to the back door from the basement and wash clothes. She would hang the clothes on the clothesline. She had one of those clothespin bags that slid along on the line. It was all different from the way things were done at home.

Her neighbors were Mr. and Mrs. Ray. They were very likable. They had a nice fenced yard and a small pug. My cousins would torment their dog by squealing PUG and the usually quiet puppy would go nuts. I heard Mr. Ray tell Grandmother that his wife slept in terrible rags. He said if he ever had to call the fire department, he would strip off her clothes and tell the firemen that she slept in the nude. In those days, I thought that little tale was a fairly risque story to tell in front of a young girl. Mama and Daddy used the term "pg" when a woman was pregnant. For some reason it was not considered proper conversation in front of children. When Mama's sister, Frances, was pregnant for the first time, she didn't want to leave the house because she said that people would know what she had been doing.

Grandmother's big house had an apartment attached to the bottom floor. At one time when I was very young Frances and Jack lived there. Then James and Tommie Sue lived there. Most intriguing was a young woman and her father who lived there. In the beginning, Grandmother had the house and the apartment separated by a curtain that attached to a big rod by large wooden circular loops. Eventually James fashioned a temporary wall out of plywood with a sliding door. The renters had a living room, a bathroom, one bedroom and a kitchen. When the people who lived there went to work, Grandmother would use their bathroom. At the time, I didn't understand why she didn't go upstairs to her own bathroom, but I understand now. The stairs were steep and she didn't want to climb the stairs unless she was headed to bed at night. Grandmother would dress when she went down in the morning and would carry her big black purse and she would stay downstairs all day long. If Grandmother needed anything from upstairs, she would send me to fetch. I didn't mind one bit.

I loved the big two story house. I adored the back bedroom. I think it used to be Tommy's room. He left his collection of John Steinbeck novels. I enjoyed stretching out in his big iron bed and reading the day away. All three sides of the room had massive windows. It felt like a tree house to me. At night I would open the windows and listen to the trains add cars. Grandmother said they were making up trains. There was lots of loud bumps, bangs, and the horns on train engines blew often. I learned to love the city sounds.

****

I got this perfect photo in the real snail mail and it gave me motivation. Thanks, Kathy Tucker.

I have painted a serious picture of our mental health rotation. It was serious business, but we also had fun. There was a fairly new athletic dorm near our entryway to Bryce Hospital and right outside it was this fountain featuring naked football gods, no doubt. I think this entire group had piled inside my old Jeep Wagoneer. Also one person was making the picture. That total would have equalled ten young women with no seats, except for the two in the front. They were piled on blankets, pillows, and their winter coats. Not what Mama and Daddy had in mind when they insured me, but it sure was fun.

I note some fellow peering out the door. Don't know if he was a student or a security guard. We left when we got our picture. We then moved to fraternity row, where we would drive through to flirt and coax some guys to follow us back to the road that took us to Bryce. Our admirers would slam on brakes just before entering the mental hospital property. We would hoot and holler and enjoy every minute. Sometimes we would unload and safely dance on the grass inside the gate. We figured they thought we were exactly where we belonged.

I spot Jeannine, Liz, Terry, Janna, and that stunning Louisa. Someone looked away and I cannot remember the girl in black with a sleeveless top. I am on the left in a car coat and light pants. My roommate, Kathy, is likely the photographer. Sweet girls acting silly and enjoying their youth. All those days were worth remembering.

****

Been thinking about the Vietnam War lately. One of my grads asked me to do an interview for her college class assignment about my opinions during some significant historical events I experienced.

I was in nursing school at University Hospital School of Nursing in Birmingham during the late 60s. I remember a sad event about the time Billy and I fell in love and got engaged.

One of my patients was a young man who made it through his time as a soldier in Vietnam, but was severely injured in an automobile accident on his way home. He had just gotten back to the U.S. and had gotten a ride home for a reunion with his young wife and his family. I happened to be working the day the doctors ran tests and determined that the soldier was brain dead. We knew to trust the test results, but this fellow showed no outward sign of injury. He simply looked like a tired guy who was sleeping deeply.

I was sorry to be on duty when the young wife and the boy's mother arrived at UAB after a long car ride. Neither of them could get their head around the fact that their loved one was gone. He was being kept alive by machines. The soldier was handsome, muscular, and tan. The family members were given 24 hours to say their goodbyes. Neither could stand being present early the next morning when the equipment was pulled. I remember standing on one side of the bed, while one of the older neuro nurses stood on the other side. We held his hands as he quietly left this world. The older nurse murmured a little prayer and thanked him for his service. The last thing she said to him was "You can rest now!"

She turned to me and said "Go wash your face. We've got a patient in the E.R. who needs this bed."

I don't understand the death of young people. I certainly don't understand war. I do know that life moves on and Life is Good!

****

The Coolest Aunt Ever

My Aunt Tommie Sue was the most with it adult I ever knew.... until I became one. She was not my blood aunt. She was the wife of Mama's brother, James Williams. We had so much in common that it seemed that we had to be related.

Tommie Sue taught me to believe that if a rule or a law or a suggestion did not include your name....it didn't apply to you. I called it her "not me" philosophy. If an elevator door said "For Employees Only", we used it. "No parking! For Employees Only" was not meant for us. She changed my life. She was not a big time rule maker or rule follower.

Tommie Sue was so good to me and she took up lots of time with me. The whole time I visited Birmingham, she planned her day around what I wanted to do. She had three boys and they just had to tag along with whatever Tommie Sue and I had planned. Uncle James drove us everywhere. Tommie Sue never drove or at least I never knew her when she drove. We would take buses where we wanted to go if Uncle James was working. Tommie Sue always had a huge purse and she had all sorts of necessities packed in that purse. Her kids seemed to always be on some type of medication. She also had a wash cloth and extra underwear and first aid supplies. She could really get mad. She would reach into the back seat and swat or pop anybody she could reach. My cousin, Jimmy, had a very smart mouth and he used it often. Tommie Sue would attempt to hit him and he would come back at her with a smart aleck comment. It was almost a little song and dance routine. I don't think that she was ever really angry and I don't think that Uncle James or any of her boys took her seriously.

Tommie Sue was a fabulous cook, but she threw things together like she cleaned house. She wasn't much of a housekeeper, but she was so much fun. When I got into nursing school, she was so handy. If I wanted tickets to a sold out concert....she always knew someone who knew someone. There was always a way. She opened many doors for me. When Billy came to Birmingham to visit me, she offered to cover for us if we wanted to spend the night together. I was too afraid of my own Mother to do that, but she would have lied for me if I had needed her to.

She had almost mystical skills. She could look at a newborn baby and somehow know immediately if the child had a physical or especially an emotional issue or a learning disability. I never dreamed of disagreeing with her.

I remember that she slept in the bed with me the night before our wedding. She told me that if you change your mind.....you do not have to marry him. I could just see her sneaking me out of the house and hiding me away in another state. No need, Tommie Sue. This was one time that I didn't need rescuing, but thanks for the offer.

Life is... Family!

Today I've been taking down my Valentines decorations. It's really quiet at my house. I've been thinking a lot about love in my family. I adored my grandparents, but I don't know that I ever heard them openly express their love for each other. My grandfather, Virgil G. Perdue, was a stern man. Mamaw, Annie Lou Folmar Perdue, told me about a time when my granddaddy had a terrible backache. She said that she had to sit on the floor and put on his shoes and socks for him. He was in too much pain to lean over. After she had laced his shoes, she said he cupped her head in his hand and said, "Ann Lou, you've been a good wife to me." She told me that was one of the sweetest things he ever said to her.

When Billy and I were married in 1968, we had our grandmothers at our wedding. He had lost his maternal grandmother who taught school in Lowndesboro for years, but the other three were in good health. When we came home from our honeymoon, Mamaw said that she knew Billy and I would have a long, happy marriage. I asked her how she knew. She said she watched him when I walked down the aisle at Luverne Methodist. She said his face just lit up. She told me that she was so glad that I had a loving, affectionate husband. I realized then that she wished my grandfather had been warmer and more demonstrative. Love is a word that flows fairly easily from today's men. Times are different now. I am blessed to have loved a man who was comfortable with expressing his feelings. I listened closely to everything my Mamaw said.

****

Life is... Family!

Our holiday season was perfect. My birthday month was fantastic. And we're 6 days into March and it has already been wonderful. March 2nd and 3rd, Julie and Bill were in Luverne on their way to the Alabama Coast. Also March 3rd is Bill's birthday and we got to spend a few unexpected hours with our entire immediate family and had a few bonus extended family members present, too. Sweet!

Friday afternoon, Chad and Mary Catherine Brooks added another precious grandchild to the Perdue clan. Jim has a pile of step grandchildren, but Vada James is the first one of his own. Billy and I have our Will, who turns 14 in a couple of weeks. Tom's Ethan Perdue has a little boy and girl, Gaige and Reed. Bob Perdue has a huge number of great nieces and nephews, but no grands yet. Being near a family newborn brought back some of the sweetest memories. Billy and I spent the weekend reminiscing about our own children and the babies on both sides of our family. Julie and Wes are both in their 40s, but our newborn memories are so clear. Also I don't think there is anything more precious than grandchildren. We have been so lucky to have Will close. I don't think I have missed many of his milestones. I wouldn't change a thing. Since we only have a single grandchild, it is such a gift to be involved in his daily life.

I remember a special family moment with my grandfather that I failed to understand when it occurred. We lived in a used, single wide trailer on the Troy Highway when we brought Julie home from St. Margaret's Hospital in the summer of 1971. My grandparents drove out to visit that very day.

I was nursing my beautiful baby girl in the back bedroom. I expected my grandmother to come into the bedroom, but I was shocked to see my grandfather over her shoulder. Virgil G. Perdue was a proper Southern gentleman. I had covered myself with a little pink blanket, but it shocked me when I saw tears in his eyes. He cleared the lump in his throat and said, "I prayed to live long enough to see this." I thought it was surprising coming from an unemotional, rather stoic man. Now I understand it so well.

Family is everything and to live to look into the faces of the future generations is a precious gift. My grandfather died about 4 years later. He did get to see several other great grandchildren added to our family. I was his first grandchild and Julie was his first great grandchild. I think it's important to add that I never detected a hint of disappointment that we weren't boys.

****

The Last Family Move to the Farm

I don't know exactly when we moved to the Perdue place. I know we were living there when JFK was assassinated. That was November 1963. I was in the 10th grade that school year. Daddy contracted out lots of the jobs and got the house built. It is on the old home spot for the Perdue Family. I remember that Thomas Ray Odum's family lived up there until Daddy tore down the old house and built the new one. When Kennedy died, that was the first tragedy that was carried around the clock on the major networks. The Space Program and the blast offs were often covered, but I don't remember any huge news tragedy until this one. We each had to get outside and pick up a bucket of pecans before we were allowed back in the house to watch the news. Probably Mama and Daddy did that so that we didn't get waterlogged with sad news or maybe they just wanted the pecans picked up. I tried to argue my way out of the work, but that didn't work.

Another strange thing we did concerning the assassination was watch Daddy take a rifle similar to the one that killed JFK and he shot a large Clorox bottle filled with water. He had measured the distance before he shot. It was dramatic and I remember that Jackie tried to pick up fragments of her husband's brain and skull from the back of the limo they rode in. Daddy's demonstration was very dramatic.

I remember getting ready for the Jr Prom at the country house. That was the 63-64 school year. My date was John Allen Butler. I had a little dressing table and a delicate stool in my room. We had beautiful hard wood floors. My little stool slid, flipped over, and I snagged my arm on the glass top on my wooden desk. The glass had been smoothed on two sides, but had been placed with the rough side out to the corner that was open....meaning not against the wall. I had to go to Dr. Kendrick's clinic, where the nursing home is now. I remember that he had a young doctor in training who sewed up my arm. It all sounds bad, but somehow Mama Mary was able to check out Martha McDougald from school. She must have really felt sorry for me because Mama got us Hince Lowe barbecue sandwiches and let us pile up and watch soap operas. Checking out of school back in the day was a huge deal. Martha did my hair and we had a ball.

I graduated in May of 1965. All of Mama's folks from Birmingham came down for the big Class Night Program. I was Class Poet, but not an Honor Student. I think Billy and I both had a high B average when we graduated. We both made exactly the same score on the ACT. He went to Troy and I went to UAB in Birmingham.

When I moved to Birmingham, Mama gave one of my brothers my room. I was homesick and would have done anything to come back home. Mama was having none of it. Years later Daddy told me that Mama said "Don't be too nice to Pat when she comes home to visit because she IS going back to nursing school." I have thanked her many times.

****

Dove Season brings back some wonderful family memories. I didn't hunt, but my Dad hunted and so did some of my brothers. When you are a kid you think other families are living life just like your family docs it. Probably not, but here's how we did dove season. Daddy would come home from a dove shoot with a bag filled with birds. He brought a big garbage can in to the middle of our den. He laid out his kill on the edge of an old blanket and divided the doves into four little piles. Each Perdue child was responsible for picking all the feathers off his/her birds. No fuss, no muss while Daddy entertained us with tales of hunters, guns, dogs, and game wardens. When all the birds were naked, Daddy took them outside and gutted and deheaded them. There was no popping out the breast. Daddy brought the dressed doves into the kitchen. He cooked them in a big pot of boiling water. He added chunks of potatoes, onions, and canned tomatoes. The soup was seasoned and in our family this southern delicacy was called dove bouillon.

The weather would have usually turned cool when the sun set. We all had gotten our baths and had on pajamas by the time the soup was ready. Mama dished up supper and we had a few saltine crackers on the side. I remember that the house smelled so good. I felt happy and secure as we all enjoyed our meal together. The doves had a few buck shot buried in the meat, but I don't remember a single one of us breaking a tooth or swallowing any metal. Times were simple in the 50's. The family rituals were comforting. Routine was pleasant, never boring.

****

I promise I am not being morbid, but Please God don't let me die at Wal-Mart! I was thinking that this morning as I was pushing a heavy cart and sweating like a pig! I think going while you are lounging on a beach chair with an umbrella drink in your hand has a much better feel to it! Just sayin'!

Since I wrote this, unless someone kidnaps me and drags me to Walmart, there is zero chance of my dying there. I drink lots more umbrella drinks. Also don't tell me you are headed to Walmart and ask if I need anything. I keep a list in my pocket. For every problem there is a solution!

****

Watching my birds feed at dusk yesterday and saw this fellow eating with them. First thought a wharf rat, but think it had a short tail or maybe no tail. Tried not to freak. What makes one thing God's Creature and another a varmint which must be destroyed? Often wonder the same about people, but I don't do politics on Facebook. Won't go there this beautiful morning.

****

Have yet another family tale. This one, of all things, about Burt Reynolds' centerfold in Cosmopolitan magazine in 1972. Billy's grandmother, Eunice Mitchell Davis, and I were very close. We were big fans of Johnny Carson and the Tonight Show. Julie was a baby who never slept. Miss Eunice was an old lady, crippled by arthritis, blessed with quick wit, and unconditional love for her grandson. She seemed to think that I was good enough for her Billy. We often watched the Tonight Show together. Julie never let me sleep and I am sure Big Mama's pain kept her up. We happened to watch the Tonight Show when Burt agreed to make this picture. We anxiously waited months for the magazine to appear. My Aunt Judy worked in Montgomery, but she came home for weekends. I was waiting at my grandparents on Friday afternoon when she drove up with the slick new magazine from a popular news stand in the city. I rushed out to the Davis Farm on the Pike/Crenshaw County line to share with my husband's grandmother. We were not disappointed. We giggled and blushed like school girls. We were silly girlfriends for a few special minutes. What fun! Yes, I have the full centerfold, but not posting to the public. I'm 70 and I don't want a Facebook reprimand. Love my family memories.

****

Oysters and Prom Dressses

What? Unlikely subjects, but significant parts of my junior high days. I played clarinet in the Luverne High School Marching Band. To be perfectly honest, I carried the clarinet and marched while others played. Long story, but related to my inability to multitask. Back in the 60s, the band had their own prom - The Band Banquet. It was held in the winter or so I think. My mother decided to make my prom dress. She was not a particularly talented seamstress. I am sure finances had something to do with her decision. She had selected purple tulle for the fabric....three shades of purple tulle. I was about 14 years old. I was not thrilled about her selection. At 14 I was very seldom thrilled about anything my parents did. Now total subject change - during this winter my family had consumed dozens of delicious raw oysters. We all loved them. Often Daddy bought a bushel or two. He washed them and iced them down. He was a skilled oyster shucker. We would gather in the back yard of the Bricken house on East First Street and have raw oysters with crackers and hot sauce. A huge family treat. We all loved those nights.

A few weeks after one of our oyster suppers, I got sick. I didn't tell Mama I had fever. I lost my appetite and felt awful. I was so sluggish. Sunday afternoon, after church, I resisted slipping into that purple prom dress for her to complete the final fitting. I finally tried it on. As Mama was adjusting the shoulder, she looked into my face. "Pat, your eyes are yellow!" She screamed. We met Dr. Kendrick at the hospital and I was admitted with hepatitis. He thought more than likely I had eaten contaminated raw oysters. I was most upset that since I had helped prepare food at a teenage party this same weekend, my friends all had to take shots of gamma globulin to protect them from the disease. A horror for a junior high age kid. Also the shots were expensive and painful. None of my friends got sick, but my brother, Tom, also developed hepatitis and shared a hospital room with me. I guess this hospital stay convinced me that I wanted to go into nursing as a career. Needless to say, I was not able to go to the Band Banquet. Years later I came upon that purple prom dress shoved in the bottom of an old trunk. I lived to tell the tale. No, I no longer eat raw oysters. Yes, I do miss them. How did Mama survive her four children? She felt guilty that she didn't realize I was sick. No problem, Mama.

****

I am so Luverne that I remember the movie theatre where Luverne Hardware is today. I remember little colored Easter chicks in the window of the hardware store on main street. I remember grilled cheese sandwiches and handmade milk shakes at both the drug stores. Also clearly remember the big fire that destroyed a whole block when we were in elementary school.

Life is... Family!

One last little post about our Destin week. This sign or one section of it makes me think of Daddy every time I see it. He was a prankster or a jokester, and a big time kidder! When he had business at the coast, he nearly always brought fish home. He would holler, "Come look what I caught!" I must have been his most gullible child. Every single time....I fell for it. Even though he was neatly dressed and there was no sign of fishing equipment, I believed he had caught a nice mess of fish. One time I noticed his little smirk. I asked, "Daddy, did you really catch these fish?" He replied, "I sure did. I gave the fish market man the money, he tossed me the fish, and I caught them!" Next time he would start the same story and I would fall for it....hook, line, and sinker! Great memories! Wonder if they made this sign just for Guy Perdue.

****

Want to share a couple of family stories about Halloween. First, as a mother, I was a total failure at the celebration of Halloween. Is it really even a holiday? Life is scary enough without a special day to celebrate fear.
At Luverne School there used to be a traditional visit of witches to the elementary school to promote attendance at the Halloween Carnival. The volunteer witches were stay-at- home mothers who

48

dressed in black clothes with pointy hats and went from class to class. Not that scary to MOST kids. Every year, kindergarten through sixth grade, I had to send a note to teachers asking them to "Please allow Julie Davis to go hide in the girls' restroom during the witches' visit." Go figure. This child also was afraid of Santa, the Easter Bunny, and terrified of the tooth fairy.

Wes was easier. He thought that it took way too much effort to dress up and travel the neighborhood for Halloween. Since Halloween fell during the harvest season, he wanted to be on a tractor or combine in some field. His idea of the perfect Trick or Treat experience was to go to the grocery store and visit the Brach's candy display. He would take one of their special white paper bags and fill it with candy. He would hand the heavy bag to me and smile and say, "Trick or Treat". I would pay for his candy and we were done until next year. Simple. No costume, no pumpkin carving, no fuss.

Love my family. We are different. Happy Halloween!

****

Another scary story, but not Halloween related. Billy and I were friends long before we fell in love. In the late summer, a crowd of us went to the old drive in theater in Luverne. The movie was The Hand and was an old horror show. This amputated human hand killed people by stabbing, shooting, and choking. A bad hand and a lame movie.

Stephen Coleman and I set up this stunt. I hid in the back of Billy's car and he gave Stephen a ride to go home and get a tennis racket. We used to have a single tennis court at the City Pool. When Stephen went inside his house, I reached from the back seat to grab Billy's throat. I must have made a noise because right before I touched Billy, he turned on the interior light and leaned over the back seat with a balled fist. He didn't think it was funny and my parents grounded me for the week.

And the man married me! He married me! We have been together almost 50 years. When I ask him WHY, he says "I didn't want a boring life." Life is Good. The heart wants what the heart wants.

Life is... Family!

The Librarian's Assistant

Miss Pat Perdue

Here's proof that I was once a calendar girl. Twelve years old and I volunteered at the library. At 18, I was the Class of '65 class poet. At 21, I married a man who loves to read. Have not advanced to really enjoying my Kindle. I love the feel of paper, the smell of old books, the magical ambience of a small bookstore and am so very proud of our outstanding Luverne Public Library. At 70, I have discovered the pleasure of a good audiobook. One reason for this new pursuit is that Billy Davis and I enjoy these books together. We do lots of riding and some nights you'll find us parked in our own driveway, finishing a great novel.

I think what pleases me most is when I drop Will at the library and later he comes out with an arm load of thick books and a big smile on his face! Passing down a good habit feels great.

****

Today was Mama Mary's birthday, June 15! We always knew we were loved and that expectations were high. Try to live up to her standards! No excuses.

****

A little remembrance from my first football season as a teacher at the NEW Vocational Center on Woodford Avenue in the late 1970's. When Luverne played Brantley, I was all decked out in my Tiger red, sitting on the Luverne side of the field. And along with the fans sitting around me, I shouted "Hit 'em. Go get 'em" until I realized that the " 'ems" were my Burnettes, my Salters, my Murrays, my Wileys, my Daniels. I had to go to the car and wait for the halftime show. Watching my new babies get hit was absolutely no fun at all! Loved my years when I taught students from Dozier, Brantley, Highland, and Luverne. There is always enough love to go around! Love this county!

****

Yet another family tale. This one is just as clear to me as the day it happened. Mama was sewing herself a red dress with big white polka dots. I was sitting watching her work. She was using her portable Singer sewing machine. I was about 10, Bob 8, Jim 5 1/2, and Tom was about 3. Bob was mowing our backyard that bordered the Luverne Methodist Church. He was using a small, quiet electric lawn mower.

I remember screams from the back yard and can see that unfinished dress falling to the hardwood floor in the den, as Mama jumped to her feet. Tom had begged to stand on the top of the mower and ride. What could go wrong? Tom's plump big toe was hanging by a tiny thread of flesh. Mama tossed Tom into the front seat of her old station wagon. There was a trail of blood through the carport. The last thing Mama shouted was "Go to Sarah's!" Sarah and Ted Bond lived across the street in the duplex. Miss Sarah washed our faces and calmed us down and gave us something cool to drink as we recounted our gruesome tale. Nothing like good neighbors. Tom was taken to Montgomery. His big toe was returned to its proper place thanks to a skilled surgeon and a metal pin. There was talk of a permanent limp. That doctor didn't know his patient was a Perdue. No limp, no noticeable scar. The day the cast came off, Tom got a spider bite on a good toe on the same foot and the beat goes on.

I soon forgot the look of my baby brother's detached toe, but I still remember Mama's unfinished red polka dot dress. Nothing easy about motherhood and a house full of rowdy kids. Rest In Peace, Mama. You earned it.

****

Life is... Family!

My grandfather had a TIA when most called it a mini stroke. He kept checking his zipper. He was such a proper man and was so worried he might expose himself. I was a nurse then. May I point out that he lived many more wonderful years and he also had an abdominal aneurysm that couldn't take surgical repair.

****

I've been thinking of a story about Mama for nearly a month. I must really need to tell this one. In the 60s my whole family went to Andalusia to Dr. King for dental care. I have deep psychological problems with dentists. I hated having anything done to my teeth, but I had a cavity that had to be fixed. Local anesthesia bothered Daddy and due to that, he thought we could all endure drilling without novocaine. Torture to me. Time stood still when I squirmed in that dental chair. I survived the visit.

Daddy and my brothers were all gone on a hunting trip that day. Mama had popped into an Andalusia grocery store while I was at Dr. King's office. When we headed home, Mama said, "Lay down and put your head in my lap if you want to." I wanted to. Mama was not a warm and fuzzy person. She did not coddle her kids. She expected us to be tough. That hour ride back to Luverne might have been one of our most significant bonding experiences ever. When we got home, Mama fixed me a very special lunch. She had bought us a pint of expensive oysters. She had a casserole recipe that was somewhat like dressing with whipping cream, crumbled crackers, butter and our oysters. When she baked it, the whole kitchen smelled so good. The food was soft as Dr. King had recommended. The very best thing about this meal was that we didn't have to share it. It was for just the two of us.

It's very hard to convey just how special this day was to me. I think it was maybe the worst of the worse and the best of the best. I guess the proof of its significance is that I remember every bit of it in such detail. Mama is long gone. I still have all my own teeth. I love oysters. I spoiled my children regularly. I ended up warm and fuzzy. We all verbalize the LOVE word. My kids type LOVE in every text, email, note. All this started somewhere. It could have started with my head in Mama's lap, on a certain day in my Southern raising. Life is Good!

Life is ... Common Ground

****

I am hung up on tomatoes this week. This morning I woke up thinking about tomato sandwiches. As kids we had lots of tomato sandwiches in the summer. We did not have BLTs. Can you imagine how many pounds of bacon it would have taken for four Perdue kids plus two parents? Also we didn't have lettuce or when we did, it was for making salads for six. I am talking about gummy white bread with mayonnaise and a slice of tomato that actually was often larger than the slice of bread. I do remember salt as the only added ingredient. Don't remember feeling deprived in any way. We were like a hoard of locusts when it came to running through groceries. My poor Mama would drag home a station wagon full of groceries and we would eat our way through it all.

For some reason today I remembered the special days when chicken was on sale for 29 cents a pound. Seems like we would stock up for the summer, but I doubt it lasted very long.

One more little family food remembrance that comes to mind. Mama used to make banana pudding before church every Sunday. I still have her bowl. I don't make banana pudding, but I often use that bowl. I think about my mother every single time I drag out that big yellow bowl. The color has actually faded, but the memories are vivid. Life is Good!

****

Folie a plusieurs

A psychological syndrome where a group of seemingly normal people developed a shared psychosis when they were together. There is always an unstable leader at the center of the sickness.... the head of the snake.

If I got rid of my demons, I'd lose my angels. Tennessee Williams

****

Life is... Family!

There's a song with a line that goes "She's like a giggle at a funeral......" That would be me. I was probably born with this tendency. I can go way back in childhood and remember many examples of inappropriate laughter. Sometimes I got spanked and sometimes I was joined by the rest of the family. The day my Daddy packed up and left home, we got tickled about a sock issue. Tom and I had a crazy moment when our beloved Aunt Judy died. It involved me falling out of Tom's truck and rolling out of sight in Daddy's back yard when we went to give him the news that his baby sister was gone. It happens.

Yesterday I had a long wait at a Montgomery doctor's office. Some other older ladies joined me in such a laugh session that one man had to leave and go stand outside to escape our joy.....or that was how one of my new friends described his behavior. He was shaking his head and fumbling around to find his smokes.

I love to laugh. It is my therapy. My sense of humor is strange, but I couldn't live without it. So if you see me in town and I am laughing....I may be laughing at absolutely nothing. I won't be laughing at you. It'll just be me being me. Life is Good. Laughter is Good.

We have such fabulous family memories in the Destin/Ft. Walton area. I guess that is why we keep returning. One time Mama took us to stay almost a full week. We went crabbing on the edge of 331 that crossed the bay. We ate ham sandwiches and drank lukewarm bottled Cokes. There were a few picnic tables along the edge of the highway. We had a few old Zebco reels on scraggly rods. We bought squid and frozen shrimp for bait. I've seldom been as happy as I was throwing live crabs into old metal buckets.

I can still hear the crabs drumming on the sides of the buckets. We were sunburned and smelly. We cooked all the crabs with corn on the cob and new potatoes and ate out in the yard of an old cabin we rented. We showered outside and put on tee shirts. The best naps were on the porch with a gentle seabreeze and crashing waves in the distance.

On the weekend Daddy came down with Coach and Ms. Gladys Sport. John and Merrill were little, bitty boys. John called the gulf the big bathtub. We had a fabulous time. On Sunday afternoon when they went home, a huge storm came up. The porch windows were almost blown in by the winds. We propped them up with mop handles and some boat oars. It was a marvelous adventure. I don't think we were scared at all.

The pictures are of a new park under the bridge. There is a boat ramp, clean restrooms, and wonderful shade. I hope children are still taken to fish, away from the amusements and water parks and get just a taste of this type family activity. I want to believe that when today's kids turn 70 that they can remember a few things that don't involve technology, air conditioning, and high dollar attractions. If that makes me sound old timey, I'm good with it!

****

I wanted to share a little story about what a good Daddy our kids have. I'd say almost 30 years ago, we were about as broke as a family could be. I was working two jobs. Billy was driving a big truck and was gone most of the week. It was the night of The Dance Center recital. When I talked to Billy about daylight that morning, I prepared myself for the fact that there was no way he could make it home for Julie's big night. I don't even know how we scraped up the money for her beautiful costumes that year, but we did. She really wanted her Daddy to see her dance, but both our kids understood sacrifice and reality.

That night the lights dimmed and the show started. I had a lump in my throat and I could feel the tears. When Julie's first dance started, I suddenly heard the most recognizable cough from the back of the CCA gym. Billy had a chronic cough since his days of picking peanuts on an open tractor. He had made it. I couldn't see him, but I could sure feel his presence.

Julie was fantastic on stage. She had the biggest smile. I so wished she knew her Daddy was there. It was a magical night and when it was all done and we were all together afterwards, she hugged her sweet Daddy. She said, "Right before the curtain opened, I heard my Daddy cough. I knew some way, somehow that he had made it. I danced my heart out for him." Life just gets no better.

Way back in the 60s, I had no clue how important it was to marry the right man. I lucked out and I found the best man to parent our two kids. No need to even mention what a good granddaddy he is. Happy Father's Day, Billy Davis. You are the man!

****

I have so few pictures with just Daddy and me. My parents had four kids and a miscarriage in seven years. That explains a lot. We really did have a wonderful childhood. I was a little bit of a wild child. I must have enjoyed bedlam and chaos. We were raised to be tough. Daddy had a certain saying that he used often. "Buck up!" We were not coddled or babied. Our parents were hard workers. Their expectations were high. We hated to disappoint them. The summer of 1968 was my most memorable summer. I graduated from nursing school in June, married in July, started my first job in August. I expected life to continue pretty much as it had been. Predictability is a warm, fluffy cloud of security and comfort. Things didn't go as planned.

Mama and Daddy split up when Julie was a toddler. Everything changed. Daddy's pledge is still stuck in my head....."I will no longer tell any of my children to buck up. I lost that right." Daddy knew he had disappointed us. We continued to love him. I had a cordial adult relationship with my father. I was no longer his little girl.

One more Happy Father's Day to my Daddy. You were a good provider and so much fun. All's well that ends well. Life is Good!

****

I know it's Throw Back Thursday. I don't have an appropriate picture, but I certainly have the memories.

About this time of year in Spring of 1978, I was a stay-at-home Mom with a seven year old and a two year old. Billy was farming. We lived in the country house that had been Billy's grandmother's on the Pike/Crenshaw County line. Billy needed to run to Montgomery for a tractor part. I asked if we could ride with him. I planned for him to drop us at Dillard's, Gayfer's, Montgomery Fair.....whatever it was called back in the day. It was the time of year to hunt for Easter clothes.

Those who know me are well aware that I do not enjoy shopping. This is nothing new. It was a chore for me. This day Billy dropped us at the store and went his merry way. We went to the children's department. I quickly located some yellow linen shorts and a white shirt for Wes. He sat quietly in his little collapsible stroller as we entered the dressing room with a half dozen pastel dresses for Julie. In those days, new children's clothes had stiff sizing and straight pins when they first arrived at stores. Julie had very definite ideas about an acceptable Easter dress. As usual, her ideas and my ideas were in different universes. I insisted that Julie try a lime green dress that would look just right with her brother's yellow outfit. Julie reasoned with me "Mama, I don't like green. Please, please, pleeeease don't make me try this one! It's green." As I slipped the scratchy garment over her head, I had overlooked one pin. It made an angry scratch on her side. Julie screamed and sobbed. Then Wes started to cry. I plopped down on the dressing room bench and joined my children in a good cry.

I left the dressing room with clothes scattered everywhere. I pushed the stroller to the exterior door and exited the store. Thank goodness, Billy had returned from his errands and was waiting in his truck. He took one look at the three of us and said "Let's go get ice cream." God bless young mothers everywhere. I don't wish to go back. This, too, shall pass.

****

Throw Back Thursday - One miserable fall in the early 60s. Some are meant to cheer and some should remain in the stands. Life lesson well learned.

Places We Lived

I mentioned that when I was a baby, Mama and Daddy lived with my grandparents. Then we lived for a while in a big house in Rutledge. The next place we lived was in a little house down at the River Bridge close to Perdue Folmar.

Life is ... Common Ground

I remember lots of little random things from my childhood. I remember that we had a next door neighbor who lived in a huge old country house next door. I think her name was Miss Glennie Sikes and she might have been related to our Mayor. She lived in half the house on the south side and she rented the north side to an old married couple. I remember spying on them with some of Daddy's hunting binoculars. That was the most boring stakeout ever. They ate supper at sunset and then played dominoes until bedtime. My venture into private investigating was short lived. I do remember one time I headed over to visit and the old gentleman was sprawled on the front steps. I was so frightened that I ran next door to our house for help....rather than attempting to help him.

I remember Dr. James Kendrick made house calls there when we were really sick or so contagious that he didn't want us in his office waiting room. I remember horrible cases of measles, mumps, chicken pox, and a zillion stomach viruses. For some unknown reason, my illnesses were much milder than my brothers. I remember my baby book and on the disease page, Mama had question marks by mumps and chicken pox for me. I think my glands were hardly swollen and I had one or two little sores. It seemed that poor Bob always had the worst case of whatever was going around. With four children, Mama taught us early to go lie on the bathroom rug if we thought we were going to be sick. There was a huge vomit pan that sat at the bedside. Sometimes when several were sick, the garbage cans from the bathrooms served us. I very seldom remember a Perdue throwing up on the floor. Daddy would light a rolled up newspaper and freshen the air in the bedrooms. I guess the smokiness was better than the vomit odor.

I am positive that we were in that house when Mama's Daddy died unexpectedly. I remember Mama sort of leaning on the door frame, clutching the phone in a hand, and then sliding to the floor. I recall the process of packing and choosing funeral clothes for her trip to Birmingham. I think Daddy didn't go and this was before Tom was born. I think Jim was a baby. We always had a local black cook, jack of all trades who was a constant with us. Lizzy was the name of the sitter when I was very young. She was young, cute , and we adored her. I remember her helping Mama pack and plan out what had to be done to keep things going. Mama was a renowned list maker. She managed to pull herself together in order to make a thorough list. I was never scared because we always had Mamaw and Duzzer to fill in. I remember Mama stayed sad for a long time. She was skinny, pale, and had anemia often. Physically Mama might have been weak, but she was extremely strong in every other way. She worked with Daddy at Perdue Folmar, what we called the shop. She kept books and kept the financial part of the business in order.

The Patsaliga River played a big part in my early childhood. I was under strict orders not to go down to the river, but I took many chances. I would lie to Mama, but usually I ruined a pair of shoes when I ventured too close to the water. I actually think that the sewers from the houses near the river dumped their waste into the river. Once I looked into our toilet bowl and there was the strangest looking, bleached out frog. I can only assume he had made the journey from the river into the bathroom. I just refused to consider that a snake could have made the same trip. There was lots of red mud and kudzu to get tangled up in. I was not scared of anything back in the day. As Mamaw said, I never believed that cow horns would hook. Amazing that I never had stitches or a broken bone until I was grown. Can't say the same for my brothers.

I remember hot summers with no air conditioning. We had window fans and in most houses had ceiling fans. I can remember shortie pajama sets that were soaked at dawn from the high humidity. The best sleep ever though with the hum of the fans.

There were many nights after supper that we sat on the front porch with Daddy, watching heat lightning in the distance. It was more beautiful than any fireworks display. We were on the edge of 331 and for long periods of time, there were no cars coming by. When they did come by, the bridge made that click-clacking noise that is still heard today.

Those nights were very special. Mama was probably inside washing dishes and who knows....maybe enjoying the peace and quiet. That was a sweet little house.

I think Daddy built the house that backs up to the Methodist Church. We lived there when there was the huge Luverne fire that took the two story hotel. It was where Angelia's flower shop is now. For a while Perdue Folmar was in the building across from Super Foods. When that fire raged, Daddy's employees emptied out the equipment into backs of farm trucks to keep from losing everything. I heard Daddy say that the men had monumental strength when that happened. One man would lift a piece of equipment alone and when the building was spared and the machines were moved back inside, it would sometimes take three men to move what one man carried out due to adrenaline and fear.

That day we could see the flames from the school yard. Somehow the school day sort of fell into bedlam. I have a clear memory of walking to town and going home. I stepped over fire hoses that were scattered all over the street. People were wet and marked with soot. When I heard that a lady died in the hotel, I knew why every adult was so down in the mouth. For years I heard the tale that Big Nit, our beloved town fat man, begged the lady to jump into his arms outside her window at the hotel. The story was that she wouldn't jump because she was not fully clothed. It became a legend in those years.

I remember playing in the backyard. Playing bride with old curtains and bridal wreath flowers. Daddy made lots of homemade ice cream. He turned the crank by hand. We played Perdue games. One was a competition where we held our hands deep in the salted ice and Daddy timed us with his watch. It always hurt too bad for me to win. I won on the ice cream eating. I still love homemade ice cream. It is one of my most favorite foods. The few times that we had leftover ice cream, Mama would put it in a container in the freezer. I would get up extra early the next morning so that I could be sure to get some. Back then it was made with raw eggs. I don't recall ever getting sick from eating ice cream. It was most definitely my comfort food.

When we lived in that house, we had the best neighbors. Ted and Sarah Bond and Jim and Bonnie Lowery lived in the duplex right across the street. I adored both of the ladies and they played big parts in my life. Every Saturday afternoon Miss Bonnie would set my hair in pin curls so that I looked fancy for church the next day. When Mr. Jim came in on the milk truck, he would nearly always have leftovers and would give us cold chocolate milk from the back of his truck. Sarah Bond was such a sweet woman. Her sister, Roslyn was gorgeous and she dated the extremely handsome Richard Brown. I loved to hang out and just watch them. Even then I was enthralled with romance.

Life is... Family!

There was a park where the Hometown Medical and Mrs Cathryn Evans' house are now. We played with scads of kids in the neighborhood. I remember one summer we had lemonade stands. I was in direct competition with Cathy and Dale Summerlin. I threatened to report them to the City Council because they were not being hygienic enough to meet standards. I had paper cups and they had real glasses. The whole process ended up in a sticky mess. We were definitely budding entrepreneurs.

Once Tommy Windham spit on me in a battle over the swings in our park. I picked up a rotten limb and cracked his head open. I just knew Miss Louise would be mad, but she said that she had told that boy not to spit on people. Daddy ordered me not to make any more of the Folmar cousins bleed. It was bad for family relationships.

Luverne Methodist had the best Bible Schools. Back then very few mothers worked and we enjoyed a full day of fun. Bible School ran for 5 days and we put on a program at church on Sunday. One year apparently the budget allowed for a professional youth leader. Woody Poole was the bomb. We adored his energetic and imaginative productions. He was something different and he was fun.

I think we moved back into the little house at the River for a while. I am positive that we lived there at the end of the 6th grade. I can see my pale pink appropriate party dress hanging on a hook in my front bedroom. Mama had a running battle with some of the other mothers. She felt that formals and dates were way too advanced for six graders. I lived for drama and I didn't agree with my mother, but I didn't tell her that.

I remember Mama hanging out clothes one pretty morning. Bob was playing with his BB gun. His pellet ricocheted off the house and embedded in Mama's back. She had a fit and used a profane word. It was not funny, but I got extremely tickled. I remember prying the pellet out of her pale, white back and struggling not to burst out laughing. Bob didn't get in big trouble, but he had to put the gun up.

Next we moved into the huge Bricken House on First Street in Luverne. I think we were renters there for about five years. I have dozens of family stories. The house was so big, but the boys slept in a huge bedroom, big enough for three twin beds with toy boxes at the foot of each bed. I remember we got the foot lockers at Rosehill Army Surplus. Daddy immediately drilled holes in each box because he knew who he was dealing with. My room was a back suite with a private bath and a beautiful view of the woods. I had a private entrance. I would never have thought of slipping out, but the opportunity was there.

I remember directing a library play of a couple marrying from the moon. I think the play was titled Wedding on the Moon. There wasn't much to it, but we put on a show in the small courtroom on a Saturday. All the parents attended and were polite about the weak script. I was most interested in the entrance of the wedding party. I think we had some space creatures and I do believe that Diane Daniel and Jim Perdue were the bride and groom. I think Mrs. Stone was the librarian and she was always in favor of creativity for her young readers.

The front sunroom in the Bricken house was big and bright. It had a red grand piano. We had a full size American flag because Mama was a Scout Leader. There was also a big tuba that Bob played in the band. At one point we had a baby rattlesnake in a gallon jug on the piano. I can still see the look on the faces of any company we had. We were an unusual bunch.

****

Part 2- Places We Lived

We lived in the Bricken house for several years. I know we were in town during the Cuban Missile Crisis. That lasted for nearly two weeks in 1962. Daddy turned the basement into a fall out shelter. I was scared, but not terrified since my parents talked it out and we had drills and family meetings to discuss the possibilities. Meanwhile at school we were having drills and classes about how to handle an attack. I was in the 9th grade. Bob was in the 6th grade and the younger brothers were in lower elementary. Daddy told us to get together and huddle in the storage room in the cafeteria until he came to get us. We didn't ride a school bus and I guess he figured that the town kids were on their own. He also said that he would have his guns in the basement and would need that to keep hungry stragglers from coming after our supplies. I don't think an 18 wheeler would store a month's supply for our drove of kids. When people ask me how I have such a good imagination.....I think the source of that gift is pretty obvious.

Jack Paar left The Tonight Show on March 30, 1962. I had pneumonia and was in the Luverne Hospital that particular night. I think we were still in town at that point.

We had a garage apartment and for a while an Iranian man and his American wife lived there. We also had our little cousin, Bonnie Bishop, live with us while her mother was dying of breast cancer in the local hospital. I have a long story about the night her mother died while she slept in the bed with me. Her mother died in October of 1958. She was 7 and I was 11. Very sad because her mother was only 33. Her brother, Dr. Mervin Perdue, came to Luverne to help his sister through this awful time. I understand that he would not leave as long as his beautiful sister was alive.

The Phillips family lived next door to us to the East. Coach Sport and Ms Gladys lived to the West of us, on the same side of the street. Earlier Reed and Susie Foster lived in the Sport house. I lugged them around like rag dolls.

On the opposite side of the street were the Copes, who owned the dry cleaners. Aunt Doris and Uncle Guy Folmar, Miss Margie Mahone, Mrs. Ellis and way down the street were Felix and Madie Horn.

I also remember that I got Hepatitis from eating raw oysters when I was in the 7th grade. I stayed in the hospital for a long time. The hospital was over where the nursing home is now. Tom ended up with the same condition and we shared a semi-private room for a while. I was 13 which meant that Tom was about 6. I remember he tormented the nurses that worked at the hospital. One time he rang the call button and then plopped a broom down right in front of the nurse when she came to see what we needed.

I remember that I lost 17 pounds then. The only time in my life when I looked frail. The day I came home from the hospital, I had taken a bubble bath and was wearing a pretty pink nightie. Daddy came in to see me when he came in from work. I remember that he bragged on how beautiful I looked. I know that he must have been shocked to see how I looked in reality. I was allowed back to school. The whites of my eyes were yellow, and even though the doctors had told my parents that I was no longer contagious, Ms. Maggie Jeffcoat cautioned the other kids to stay away from me. I just kept on plugging along. I don't feel scarred by this, but I dang sure remember it.

****

I thought every family did this. I remember going to the back woods with my granddaddy, Duzzer, and later going with my Daddy to shoot a little piece of mistletoe from the tip top of some huge oak trees. Just part of Christmas in the South; shooting down mistletoe with a rifle made perfet sense.

****

Old Maid Aunts

Billy and I both had aunts who had never married and never had children. That provides a special situation for nieces and nephews.

Billy's Aunt Frances Martin lived in Lownesboro. She was a huge woman with a large frame and carried lots of extra weight. I liked her from the first time I met her. She was so very generous that you had to be careful about complimenting a scarf or a necklace or anything that she could take off and hand to you. I have heard that said about many, but it was really true about her.

She and her mother lived together. I only saw Billy's maternal grandmother a few times. She was in a nursing home in Montgomery about the time we became engaged. We picked up Frances to take her out to dinner when we visited Billy's grandmother. I got in the back of Billy's car and we gave Frances the front, passenger seat. It was cramped and she pushed back and just destroyed the underpinnings of her seat. From that night on, when I rode with Billy, when he put on brakes the seat would sling me forward and then when he took off from a stop light it would sling me backwards. We always laughed and it didn't really bother us all that much.

Life is... Family!

The Davises had an outdoor swimming pool way back before
that was common. Frances would often swim with us. She had a
gigantic black bathing suit. We would float in the cool water and
relax on summer afternoons. One day this snake stuck its head
over the edge of the pool to get a sip of water. We all immediately
exited the pool. Frances was fast on her feet and we always
laughed that it seemed that she pulled about half the water in the
pool out with her.

Once Frances was admitted to the hospital in Montgomery. Both
her sisters were quite certain that the doctor would chastise Frances
about her weight and put her on a strict diet. Frances was ready
and when the doctor entered her room, she immediately told him
that she was on a diet and to make certain that the kitchen did not
send her any fattening food. I loved that she out thought them all.

At Christmas, Frances would come down on Christmas
morning and would have several extra large shopping bags from
Montgomery Fair or Gayfers or wherever. When it was her time
to gift, she would pull out an item....say for instance....blue kitchen
towels and would ask...Now who has a blue kitchen? She never
wrapped or labeled anything, but we were always happy with her
gifts and the way she presented them.

She always hit the stores at the last minute on Christmas Eve.
She came one Christmas with metal, engraved ornaments that
had been trashed. She had some marked with names that did not
match anyone in our family.   My kids thought that was so funny
that they would always claim the mismatched, flawed ornaments.
Memories to laugh about.

****

My post yesterday about my love of reading has moved me to
make a minor confession from high school days. I was in the
marching band and was listed as a clarinet player. Truth be told,
I toted a clarinet. Never did learn to play my instrument. One
reason being that I started reading Gone With the Wind. I read late
into the night, but I finally had to sleep. I took the book to school
and during band practice.....I did a bad thing. I took a pencil and
gouged out the pad of one of the clarinet keys. The poor band

director had no clue as to how low I would stoop to get reading time. He glued the pad into its proper location. He gave me the news that it needed to dry for 24 hours. Too bad, so sad! My, oh my, whatever could I do with my hour scheduled band practice? He parked my sorry butt right outside the band room in a folding metal chair. For a precious hour, I joined Rhett and Scarlett in the old south. Never did get into clarinet, but I loved to read then and I love to read now. We have some fine musicians in our family. I am not one.

When Tom was a little boy, he used his night time prayers as a technique to postpone bedtime. When he completed, Now I Lay Me Down to Sleep and moved past immediate family to extended family and friends.....he resorted to God Bless Mamaw's old green cat. Hey, Tom Perdue, I found your fantastic feline. You are so creative. Love you, Baby Bro!

****

We had a very enjoyable Book Club meeting at Luverne Public Library yesterday. We talked about books, of course, and drifted into discussing children who love to read. Then we talked about how many types of educational experiences are available for kids now. Public, private, home schools along with techno tutoring in every imaginable area appear to be thriving.

Somehow it just popped out of my mouth that Mama Mary used to check me out of school on the days that Mamaw killed chickens on the farm. It was my own private, educational field trip way back in the early 1950s. That was when I became so intensely and actively involved in the study of anatomy and physiology. I found out quickly that the sight of blood didn't bother me in the least. I wanted to identify and learn the parts and the functions of every inch of a chicken. Apparently having a rather unusual and curious female child did not alarm my mother or my grandmother.

Also remember Pat Walker, Stephen Coleman and I dissecting a snake we had killed on the wide brick wall behind the Bricken house on East First. All that obviously came to nothing.

Well, the rest is history. I survived nursing school back in the olden days. Came home, worked in health care and ended up teaching school for over 25 years. My point to this ramble is that you never know where the journey begins. Life and careers do not come with a road map. Children arrive without instructions attached. Go with it. Sometimes things just fall into place when you give kids some room.

****

Beautiful MLK Day! Hope my teacher friends are cuddled up and sleeping in. I told you last week that a rat had joined my fine feathered friends on the deck. I have another tale to share.... imagine.

When we lived in the big Davis house on the Pike/Crenshaw County line, I got up early one cold morning to turn on the coffee maker. I was shocked to see some tiny mice scatter to hide under the stove eyes. Nasty, right? Except these little bitty creatures had Mickey Mouse ears; exactly the shape of the traditional Mickey ears we brought home from Disney World the year before. I just couldn't go after Mickey with rat poison. Also these were too small to be caught with a traditional rat trap. This was long before the availability of sticky traps. What to do? What to do?

After Billy left for work, I plotted and planned how to solve the Mickey issue. I located a huge wine jug with a big mouth and a long neck; surely not emptied by me. I tilted the bottle to the edge of the sink. I baited it with some tiny bites of cheddar cheese and created a trail on the counter top to the mouth of the jug. I tossed a few pieces of cheese into the bottle neck. I turned off the kitchen lights and went on with my day.

Amazingly my plan worked. The bottle was full of little Mickeys and I assume a few Minnies. Capture successful. I put the cap on the jug and carried my cargo to the backside of a field several hundred yards from the house. I released the critters. M-I-C-K-E-Y M-O-U-S-E was playing in my ears. I returned home with a smile, while whistling It's A Small World. The moral of this story is that you might escape a sad ending due to something as simple as having cute ears.

****

A Bra Story

Back when I was a senior high student at Luverne High School, I went home to pick up a few items for a project that was due that day. Mama wasn't real big on baling us out in situations like this. I was in that bottom on Woodford where Hick's Tackle is now located. I was driving with the window down on the driver's side. I felt a flutter down in my blouse. I looked down and there was a huge black wasp sitting on that band right in the middle of my bra. I slammed on brakes and snatched my blouse open. With the back of my hand, after several attempts, I whisked the critter away.

I gulped a deep breath and started to button up my blouse when I noticed a black gentleman who had stopped dead in his tracks and had obviously witnessed my insect induced seizure. This was the 60s when there was very little interaction between males and females of different races. I realized that this man probably assumed that young white women were prone to public fits. I smiled, said "Gotta get to school" and drove away in my little blue Studebaker.

There was no adequate way to change his opinion. Just somehow needed to tell this. And if your grandad told you this story of a crazy white woman in the south....It was me!

More Bra Stories

A few months after Will was born, I was lugging him around and realized that the underwire in my bras was stabbing me in the chest. I just couldn't tolerate it. I bought several soft, comfortable sports bras.

I commented to Billy that the new bras felt so much better. He commented that I sure did look good when I wore the underwire. Big Mistake!

I told him that maybe he should get a jock strap with underwire so that he could lift and separate and look like he did as a 20 year old. He said, "I knew better. I should have kept my mouth shut."

Bet he won't do it again.

Reminded me of another story. When I was younger and still teaching, I started getting up and walking before work. I bought a couple of sports bras that slipped over my head. The first morning I put one on, I took a long, brisk walk. When I got back home and headed to shower, I absolutely could not get the wet thing off. I finally had to wake Billy up and get him to help me remove it. I didn't want to cut it, since it was new, but I ended up giving it away and in the future I only bought sports bras with a clasp.

The Ingram Girls had a party at their house in the summer between the 6th grade and the 7th. I wasn't wearing a bra then because I didn't need one. Those were the olden days. Thin, white cotton blouses with big ruffles were very popular. You could see right through these tops. Mama made me wear a sleeveless tee shirt that belonged to one of my brothers. Not the way I wanted to look, but there was no rushing Mama.

Happy Friday! I promised two grandmother stories and here they come.

I loved Billy's paternal grandmother, Eunice Mitchell Davis. She loved Billy so much that she thought he was slim. She also felt that I was good enough for him. Amazing to me, even after 50 years. Soon after we married, I was visiting with her in the back yard. I noticed there were men's white boxers hanging on her clothesline. Her husband had been dead for at least 20 years. That night I asked Billy about the underwear. He said the boxers had belonged to his granddad. I said, How romantic! I thought it was her way of staying close to her deceased spouse. He laughed and said, "I don't think so. Poppa had just ordered a dozen of his favorite drawers right before he died and Mama does not believe in waste." I think my take on this was much sweeter.

Mamaw, Annie Lou Folmar Perdue, was the most influential adult during my childhood. I am turning 70 soon and I still think of her daily. One afternoon I stopped by her house for a quick visit. She was pressing a stack of my granddad's boxer shorts. "Mamaw, what in the world?" She laughed and explained that Duzzer was going for weekly shots at Dr. James Kendrick's office. "I am pressing these because Miss Alice Curtis sees these shorts when Virgil drops his pants for his shot. Your granddaddy has a crush on Alice and well, you see..."

I love family stories. I hope you do, too. It's not all about bras. There is nothing like family.

Life is... Family!

I love celebrating motherhood, but raising a family is certainly not all sunshine and roses. I woke up early this morning thinking about a day when I pitched a huge hissy fit. I think Wes had turned 3 and that would make Julie almost 8. We had stopped at the grocery store after a tough spring day at school. I remember unloading the car and making a flying trip to the bathroom. I had put Wes in his little sandbox with his John Deere tractors and told Julie to keep an eye on her brother. We had a nice fenced yard under huge pecan trees. Five minutes later, I looked out the back door and saw Wes playing with a barn cat that was literally foaming at the mouth. I grabbed my sweet baby boy to put him in the tub and to look for signs of a bite or a scratch. I told Julie to stay at the back door and watch the cat until I could get back. I gave her these instructions in my most panicked tone.

I stripped off Wes's play clothes and scrubbed him in the warm water. I was shaking like a leaf. I was thinking rabies and dangerous treatments. I didn't see a mark on him. I wrapped him in a towel and ran back outside to deal with the situation.

No sign of the cat. I asked Julie, "Where is the cat?" She said, "Mama, it just disappeared." Now this was long before cell phones. All the men were working in the fields. I clutched my sweet baby in my arms and did what any young Southern mother would do.....I screamed and cried and I didn't stop screaming until someone came to my rescue. I had lost it, in every sense of the word.

Dot McLeod, our next door neighbor, promptly showed up in our back yard. She had a house full of kids and was the calm force that I so desperately needed at this moment. She located the cat and put it in a box. Somehow Billy had gotten word that his wife had gone insane and had come in from work. We took the cat to Dr. Doug Hawkins in Troy. It did not have rabies, but we did pay him to hold the cat for observation. It had been injured. He treated the animal and placed the cat with a more stable family. For weeks Julie repeated, "That cat just disappeared." This long story is one more reason that I will always love the Tucker/McLeod family. Yes, Mother's Day is a wonderful celebration. Just keeping it real.

Life is ... Common Ground

I'm going to make an obvious statement. We are all going to get old unless we tragically die young. The lady in this old picture is my maternal grandmother. I think I look most like her. I write a lot about my Perdue grandmother. We were very close. I only got to see my city grandmother a few times a year. I loved Birmingham. Grandmother Williams was a sports fan. She was nosy. She had a great imagination. She loved to read and listen to the Birmingham Barons on her radio. Also that strap is from her slip. She wore bras on Sunday and I assume to funeral services. Not a fan of the bra!

Today as I was scanning Facebook, I noted that I had mistakenly posted something about flower pots and potting soil on the page about an honor that Luke Boyd had been awarded. I wrote Lori Boyd and attempted to explain my error. I think it is very difficult to adequately cover one's senior moments, brain farts, or whatever cute term you choose. Nothing about it can be hidden. To you people who say that age is just a number.....well, tell that to my knees. I've got lots of good company in my journey over this hill. I very seldom spend more than a few moments with a fellow golden ager before one of us forgets a name, loses an item, or needs to hunt a restroom. Have you noticed all the laughter that seems to be generated by a group of old folks? That's my most favorite thing about age. So much of life is funny. Also note that nothing shocks or surprises us. We go with the flow. My advice and you didn't ask for it.....Don't fear age. Embrace it. Expect to mess up! Life is Good!

****

National Sisters Day! Ooopppss! I called Tom "Sue" when he was born and dressed him in frilly clothes, but that didn't work at all. Mama Mary called a halt to that foolishness in a few weeks and here we are 60 years later. Total failure, but I do love my bros most days!

****

Since today is Pi Day I feel compelled to share a math story. When I attended Luverne High School and was somewhat lazy and unmotivated, I did not apply myself to Algebra II, which Mrs. Trubie Merle Strickland taught. I failed the course. Well, actually my Daddy removed me from the class when it was obvious I would not pass. Two senior math credits were a minimum requirement for application to nursing school.

Due to my actions or failure to act, I had to move to Birmingham for the summer to take an advanced math class at Ensley High School. There were no summer classes, no second chances offered in Crenshaw County back in the sixties. I was forced to live with my Grandmother Williams. My Uncle James dropped me at Ensley School in the mornings on his way to work, but in the afternoons I had to take a city bus to get home. I also had to endure a bus transfer and finally walk three city blocks to get home. We covered a week's work in a school day. Which also meant I had to do homework all afternoon.

I really did miss my Luverne life with the City Pool, the summer slumber parties, and sleeping late. I was a country girl and way outside my comfort zone.

As my friend, Dr. Jane Lamb, says to teenagers, You pay now or you pay later. I grew up that summer. I realized for each decision, there are consequences. Life lessons well learned. Today, Pi Day, I honor mathmatics to the fullest.

My Aunt Judy

An Old Maid Aunt is a tremendous asset for her nieces and nephews. She has no kids of her own and due to the fact that she has no kids, she has more money than the other aunts and uncles. She doesn't spend too much time around kids and we were a treat to her.

Judy Perdue was Daddy's baby sister. She was always skinny and graceful and attractive. She had some relatives and friends who were also childless. Judy was especially close with her first cousin, Macy Folmar. For years they lived in an apartment, in the top two rentals, but separated by hallways and stairs. I never would have expected Judy to have a roommate. She wasn't that crazy about people and she needed down time.

I was the first grandchild and Judy spent lots of time with me. As I got older, I got to spend time with Judy in Montgomery. She worked at the Archives and History Department. I guess she was a secretary, but we thought that she ran the place. I think her job allowed her plenty of time to entertain a talkative little niece. I loved the elevator in the department. That was back in the day that there were elevator operators. The elevator operators at the Archives and History were prison trustees. I loved the drama of that and rode that elevator all day long.

Judy would take me to Morrison's and let me order any and everything I wanted. She only got a glass of tea because she knew I would never eat all that I ordered. She often bought me a cute little dress and she bought fresh bing cherries, just because I loved them. She wanted me to be happy.

When I grew up and married Billy, she was the person at the wedding who handled the brides book and signed in the guests. She didn't act like she wanted to do this, but she didn't refuse me. I remember that she visited me when I had the kids at St. Margaret's Hospital....right down the street from her office. I named our daughter after her. When I had Wes, she worried that I was going to name him Jed and she lobbied hard for another name. She said that she would always think of Jed Clampet on The Beverly Hillbillys. I decided to name him after his great grandfather, Seaborn Wesley Martin. It all worked out.

Judy always loved cats more than she loved people. I was good with that. One of my sweetest memories was dancing with her in Mamaw's living room. She had a stereo and classical records. She loved to dance and I wrapped myself in old white sheer curtains and whirled and twirled to the music. I didn't know another person quite like Judy Perdue. There ended up being six of us, three boys and three girls. I'm sure she loved us all, but I felt extra spoiled and petted when it came to Judy.

Judy smoked, but never in front of her father. I would sit with her and Mamaw on the front porch on Friday nights and talk and mostly listen to tales of old times and the Folmar family. I can see her on the front porch, in the glow of her cigarette, while I was in the swing with Mamaw. Some of the best times ever. I finally outgrew those nights when I entered high school and began to go to ballgames and started to date. I stayed close to Judy until she died. I used to call her at night and just chat. Once Mamaw had died, Judy had her stove removed from the house in town. She cooked on a hot plate and mostly microwaved her food. She was much more interested in feeding her felines than she was in feeding herself.

She became known as the Cat Lady in Luverne. She had feeding stations and fed and looked after cats. She did a brisk business at the local vet's. At home she had cats who visited her outside the fence. Then she had cats worthy of the back yard. Finally she had inside cats who were royalty. Her house smelled like cat urine, cat food, and cat love. Not a fun place to visit in her later years. My Daddy went over every single night to visit about sundown. I wonder if I have a single brother who would visit with me under these unpleasant circumstances.

My Aunt Judy is cremated and buried at the feet of Mamaw. So appropriate! I ride by and speak several times a month. She was loved by cats and nieces!

****

My brother, Bob Perdue, and I are hung up on sharing bicycle tales. I only had one bike. Got it one Christmas - used and painted it blue. It was my transportation on the east side of Luverne for years. My mother was a dancer and she tried to make me into one. I was forced to take dance lessons. I took dancing from some of the different instuctors who taught through my younger years. My last classes were with Sylvia and Jane Watson. I liked the Watsons, but I didn't like the dancing. Mama even arranged for private, summer classes. Torture for me and probably equally painful for the Watson girls. I always attempted to "forget" my scheduled dance lesson, but that ploy never worked with Mary Perdue. Mama was a renowned list maker and she would punch me up in plenty of time to go down the street for my class. This particular day I slipped my dance bag over my handlebars and struck off to the dreaded dance class. About the time I was in sight of the Watson's house, that dance bag slipped between the spokes of the front wheel and without warning that old blue bike and this reluctant dancer flipped end over end down First Street. I had the breath knocked right out of me and I had some tiny bits of gravel buried in my palms. Truth be told, I wasn't really hurt. Secretly I wished for some blood or at least some obvious evidence of injury. I walked my bike on to the Watson's. They sent me to the bathroom where I washed up and collected my thoughts. I looked in the mirror over the sink, but I just couldn't see that dancer that Mama imagined. That day we went on with my scheduled lesson. Finally Mama gave up and quit throwing her money away. I also never went on to become a female Lance Armstrong. Moral of this story is that mothers have their dreams, but daughters have their limitations. A generation later, Mama got her dancer and the rest is history.

****

Pat as a town kid

My most vivid memories as a child come from the years when we lived in the huge Bricken house on First Street. We lived there when I had my first real boyfriend, David Edgar. He moved here and lived here several years. He was very cute and we were enthralled with each other. He was allowed to come sit in the sunroom with me when Mama or Daddy were home. We were a very innocent little couple. When David's family moved, I was devastated. It just so happened that we were having a big revival at First Methodist Church when I learned of the move. David had been drafted into the choir. I was sitting on the back seat of the main sanctuary on the left side of the church. I started crying and just totally lost control. Many of the older ladies of the church thought that I was in the midst of some intense religious experience. Mama eyeballed me and whispered, "I am going to kill you when we get home." She didn't kill me, but she thought that I was being overly dramatic. It just broke my heart for my first junior high boyfriend to move away.

The Bricken house had a garage apartment. I had several slumber parties while we lived there. It had a kitchen and a little bathroom. I remember one party where we cooked brownies. We dyed some fudge icing green and made a perfectly shaped cow pattie in the middle of the pan of brownies. It was just gross enough to appeal to a crowd of young teenage girls.

The property also had a pretty little playhouse. I remember that we all played there often. Once when Susie Foster lived next door, she and her sister Reid were playing with me, I heard the distinctive sound of a falling limb high in one of the huge pecan trees. Susie was maybe 4 years old. I reached out and pulled her to my chest. We were wedged against the play house when the gigantic limb crashed to the ground. None of us were injured. When Daddy walked down after work to eyeball the limb, he looked stunned. He realized that it could have killed any one of us. I never knew what made me aware enough to grab the child.

We had big Christmases there. The tree was always in the front room so that the tree showed from the road. This was back in the day when one light went out on the string of Christmas lights.... they all went out. We used live cedar trees that we cut up on the farm. Nothing compares to that smell. Artificial trees are grand and easier, but real trees smell like Christmas. We got lots of junk on Christmas. Santa never wrapped our gifts. We usually got one or two nice gifts and then a pile of mess. Four children around a Christmas tree was a party.

I learned to cook a little bit on weekends in that town house. I had a little Golden Book that had simple recipes for children. My favorite recipe was corn bread. It had a little sugar added. We ate it with butter and it was totally delicious to me.

I could cook hamburgers and I could make chicken salad. Anything fancy was made by our black maid/cook/nanny during week days. Mama did not believe in any junk food in her kitchen. I know that we ate up salad makings, before she could make a green salad. We loved celery, plain lettuce, and we would eat lemon and salt. Mama also did a Sunday lunch after church. For years and years Mama made a banana pudding on Sundays. She actually did cook a custard that was poured over the bananas and vanilla wafers. Some mothers made a meringue on their banana puddings. Not Mama! She had a certain yellow bowl that she served it in. I still have that bowl and I always think of Mama when we use the bowl. We were lucky to get cooked custard and not instant vanilla pudding. Mama worked in the Perdue Folmar office. She considered herself a business partner. She did not mark her worth by her housekeeping or her cooking. Mama was a smart woman and she made certain that we knew it.

We had a big freezer that sat in the playroom. Mama and Daddy bought the freezer and a food plan that went along with it. The food was horrible. No matter how long you cooked the vegetables....they were crunchy and bright green. We got food delivered in dry ice once a month. As soon as the plan was done, Mama and Daddy never signed up for that type plan ever again. We ate the food. We complained and we laughed, but we ate the food.

Mamaw and Daddy's sister, Judy, often came to eat with us on Saturday night. Duzzer never came. He ate cereal early and never left the house at night. He always had a nice physique and never got plump. He was a hard worker and he got plenty of exercise. We loved having Saturday night company. I remember we watched TV and sometimes played a board game. We ate oysters, pancakes, and sometimes grilled hamburgers.

Mother had a hard time on school mornings getting us all four out the door on time. I remember one morning, to prove a point, Mama left me and Tom. She drove off and left us. We took money out of our Piggy banks and called Mr. Yates, our local taxi man. When Mama drove up from delivering her good kids, Tom and I waved as we were being driven to school by the taxi. Mama told me that she felt like she had been kicked in the gut. I thought she should have been proud that she raised children who could think on their feet. I did not actually say that because I knew how to interpret that look on her face.

Daddy had a matched set of registered beagles. When the female came into heat, every dog in Luverne city limits was interested except our male, Rex. Ol Rex just didn't give a rip. Daddy consulted with our vet, Dr. Warren Williams. He sold Daddy some attraction spray that was labeled Bitch Spray. There was absolutely no nasty talking allowed at the Perdue House. We laughed and laughed about the Bitch Spray. I remember showing some of our neighbors Daddy's latest purchase. Daddy finally gave up and sold the female. We kept Rex, but he never developed an interest in females. Figure that out for yourself.

There was a huge tragedy when we lived in that house. During the Christmas holidays, for many years, the City of Luverne would have lines of Christmas lights across our streets. Somehow late on a Friday afternoon, Mama struck Mr. Welch and he was killed in front of the Luverne Post Office. Mr. Welch worked at Lisenby Shoe Store. He helped fit our shoes when we were little. We all liked him and thought he was a special person. Mama was so distraught over this accident that Dr. Kendrick put Mama in the hospital for a night or two. I think that Mr. Welch stepped out in front of her and he was not crossing at the corner. It was a dark, wintery night. It changed things in our family. It took Mama a very long time to get over the accident. Several years later, Mama hit a dog just down first street from our house. She had a breakdown and was screaming and crying. I think somebody called Daddy and he came and got her. Someone took us on to school. That was not a time when families took school attendance lightly.

****

Thinking of simpler days....when Spring Break was AEA, when a day trip to the public park at Ft. Walton was a vacation extravaganza, and when beach supplies were a bath towel and one bottle of suntan lotion. We took sandwiches and a few drinks. If we fought, whined, or begged, we were brought home early. Thank God for a simple Southern raising.

****

Yesterday when we took a long, country ride, we passed a home place I used to visit when I was a young, newly married, recently graduated nurse. The paint was not as fresh and there were a few patched roof spots. At that time, I was the only Public Health nurse in the county and was as green as grass.

I visited an old gentleman in that house. He had a sweet little wife who was probably a tad younger than he was. She was in lots better shape than her husband. My patient had suffered a stroke. He did not talk. He didn't seem to be aware of much. He wore a bib that his wife had made from a cheap hand towel and grosgrain ribbon. The man drooled and dribbled grits and butter as his wife fed him. She tenderly held a coffee cup to his cracked lips between bites. He was neatly shaved. His hair was combed. I could catch a whiff of Old Spice aftershave.

The wife had turned the living room into a sick room. Her husband had a hospital bed. There was an old iron frame double bed pushed into a corner. There was a pretty blue quilt that served as a bedspread. The room was neat and clean. As I checked my patient's vital signs and looked at his thin ankles for swelling, I commented to his wife that he looked like he had lost weight since my last visit. She agreed with me. She chuckled and said, "I wish you could have seen him in his prime. A hell of a man! Wish our little boy had lived. He would have been a handsome fellow."

Then she made a comment that surprised me , "I guess if he were still a big man, I'd have a mighty hard time sliding him over into our bed every night." "Really?" I blurted. She answered, "I know he can't have much longer with me and I just really enjoy cuddling up with him. I want every night I can get."

I left in a little while. I charted the medical information and drove off to see my next Home Health patient. Every single time I ride past that spot, I remember when I learned something new about true love.

****

This picture of an old gas space heater made me remember undoubtedly the coldest winter of my life. After Christmas holidays, in January 1967, part of my nursing school class started psychiatric nursing classes at Bryce Hospital in Tuscaloosa. We lived in a dorm inside the gates of the hospital. We did our clinicals on the wards of Bryce. The limited winter warmth was provided by giant space heaters, just like the one in this picture. We wore street clothes, not nurses uniforms. We were not allowed to wear pants. At that point in time, pants were not considered appropriate attire for young women.

If I were to select a particular moment when I became an adult, I honestly believe it was during this month. I learned a lot about mental health and I learned even more about humanity. I met some seriously disturbed individuals, but I also got to know people who had landed in a mental hospital by rotten luck and a legal system that ran out of options. Huddled in front of sputtering gas heaters, with nothing to do but talk, I heard the life stories of people astonishingly similar to me and the people I grew up with. My eyes and my heart were opened in more ways than I can list. Thankful this morning for a warm house, a good family, and having had experiences that made me who I am.

****

Talking with a friend this morning about being grateful. Reminded me of some tough times we had way back when. Before the term Farm Crisis was dreamed up, we were struggling. Billy was working as hard as was humanly possible. I was teaching all day and doing contract work for home health every weekday afternoon. Our kids were doing their homework by flashlights in the back seat of our rattle trap brown station wagon while I visited patients on some muddy back roads. Not exactly living the dream.

One winter afternoon, I drove down a bumpy trail to a little frame house with rickety steps and a tin roof. In this front yard was a hound dog who always perked up and started his tail wagging and friendly yapping when he spotted us. Julie, in her infinite wisdom, rolled her brown eyes at me and laughed and said, "Mama, you do know that you just waved at a dog." All three of us burst into laughter and I knew then that we were going to make it. Merry Christmas and Happy New Year to You and Yours!

****

That frost last week got my pretty blooms on my single bridal wreath that my kids gave me for Mothers Day a couple of years ago. It didn't take my memories.

When I was an upper elementary girl, we lived in the house that backs up to the west side of Luverne Methodist Church. The back yard was bordered by a thick wall of bridal wreath bushes. Back then girls seemed to have great imaginations and limited commercial resources. Nicely put, actually our parents could not afford costumes and expensive toys. We didn't need them. We didn't have them.

One spring Saturday, Lucile Duncan was invited for a play day. We hit that back yard with some old sheer curtains and a pack of bobby pins. We spent the whole day playing bride. There were long pieces of the bridal wreath pinned in our hair. We made our own elaborate bouquets and fashioned a beautiful aisle bordered in bridal wreath limbs. I know one question pops up from friends who grew up with us. Where were the rowdy Perdue boys during all this? The one time they showed up, I posed them for mock wedding pictures on the back stoop leading down to our ceremony. I would take my hands and move their faces this way and that to achieve the perfect angle. The first time I stopped to reload my imaginary camera..... poof, they disappeared! Guys were really not that important for wedding play. Later I heard them in the midst of an impromptu football game in the front yard.

This scenario is etched in that special childhood corner of my aging brain. Even today, some 60 years later, I never pass a bridal wreath bush without smiling. There were no pictures made or no big commemorative keepsakes preserved. No need.

Hope Leslie Helms, Lisa Rolling, and my daughter Julie read this and catch a glimpse of your mothers as Southern girls in their element.

****

One more Mother's Day related story I need to share. When Julie was a toddler and Billy was away on a truck, someone played a prank on me and was banging on my bedroom patio door late at night. I called my grandmother when I first heard the noise and thought it was coming from outside. When I realized it was in the bedroom, she grabbed her sawed off shotgun and was headed across the pasture that was between her house and mine.

Thank goodness I finally realized it was a foolish joke. I remain glad that she didn't kill the person messing with her grandchild and first great grandchild. She had fire in her eyes and she was coming to save us. I loved my Mamaw! I knew she was dangerous when it came to family. By the way, the gun was a snake-killing gift that my Daddy gave her for Mother's Day. Happy Mother's Day and no, I don't expect to receive a gun today!

My Mamaw - Annie Lou Folmar Perdue. This little woman was the strongest influence in my life. Period! If you needed to research unconditional love, she would be a good place to start. I was her first grandchild. She made me feel special. She also made me feel rich, smart, and unique. I really don't remember wasting any of our together time worrying about being pretty, proper, or prissy.

She treated me like she treated my brothers. Obviously she was a woman ahead of her time. If I have a legacy, it would be knowing that Will Davis remembers me when he's 70 years old and a granddaddy himself. Life is Good! Family is everything!

****

This recollection started when someone mentioned tumbling classes at LHS. This had to have occurred after PE requirements dropped the bubble suits and advanced to white shirts and red shorts. Think they had snaps instead of buttons. Also believe our names were monogrammed on the shirts. I remember that these outfits stunk or at least mine did. The very last thing on my mind was taking my gym clothes home on Friday afternoons to wash them. There were showers in the girls dressing room, but I only recall them being utilized to change clothes in private.

We were having tumbling and the mats were stretched out so that we had a long runway for acrobatics. My single skill was a forward roll, better known as a somersault. I never advanced past this rudimentary move. The majority of us dreaded these classes. One weekend after five days of tumbling, I developed a very red, itchy patch on my lower back. The more I clawed, the larger this grew. Mama took me to Dr. Kendrick after school on Monday. As soon as he took a look, he asked if I had PE. Of course, the answer was Yes. He asked if I had been on the mats. I told him Every single day last week. His diagnosis was ringworm. He said the football team uses the mats for rests and naps prior to football games. He said that presently the Luverne Tigers had the worst outbreak of athletes foot and jock itch in the history of the school. Yuck! Gross!

He prescribed medication and gave me a three day excuse from PE. I was mortified and to make a bad situation worse, the Perdue Boys quickly formed a trio and sang the following to the tune of Camptown Races:

Pat's got a ringworm on her butt.
Doo-da, Doo-da.
Pat's got a ringworm on her butt.
Doo-da, Doo-da
Goin' to itch all night
Goin' to itch all day
Bet yo money I'm gonna tell
It ain't goin' away.

I recall some minor bloodshed that did not require stitches. Maybe a black eye or a busted lip.

You can't make this stuff up! Have a good Monday and thank goodness for Clorox wipes and Lysol. There is fungus among us! It's funny now!

****

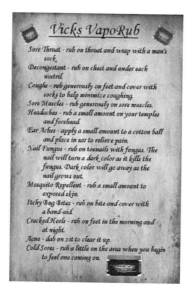

Vicks Vapo-Rub was Daddy's go-to treatment for kids with bad colds. First he would insist that we take a hot bath with the shower curtain closed in order to breathe the steam. When we were settled into bed, he would arrive with that familiar blue jar. He would briskly apply the Vick's to the chest. There was no way to avoid that final, swift swipe of the goo under the nose. I don't know if this actually helped, but he tried. The things we remember and the people we miss. I wouldn't mind him showing up to help me out with this crud. I'm not doing grown up today.

* * * * * * * * * * * * * * * * * * * *

Tales from Old Luverne

I adored swinging on summer nights on my grandmother's porch swing and listening to her tales of the old days in Luverne. She told me of how popular pranks were when she was a kid. She told a lot of stories about young people scaring drunks and other kids and somewhat intellectually slow people. She told of people crawling out of freshly dug graves. About making scary noises. And stories of stuffing cotton hose with newpaper and tying it with fishing line so that it was drug through the grass and made to look like a snake. Things have really changed, but I can so imagine modern day kids getting in serious trouble about such shenanigans.

Daddy loved to tell this story to his big eyed kids. He said that if you took a big butcher knife to the grave yard and asked the deceased what they were doing...they would say Nothing. I fell for that story every single time.

I guess we were easily entertained. Sometime we would argue for an hour about if a tree falls in the woods and no one was around to hear it fall, did it really make a noise. We would sometimes pass licks of that one.

She also told me that courting couples had lots of privacy. There were often picnic dates when a wagon was borrowed and two or three couples would ride out to some pretty spot for their picnic. She said that there were no adults around for miles. I had never thought of that before.

She told me that she once rode out to the Davis Farm with her Dad or maybe one of her uncles. She said that Eunice Mitchell was a little older than her and that she complimented her bonnet. Miss Eunice, Billy's grandmother, later told me the same thing. My grandmother was such a Tom Boy that I couldn't imagine her wearing a frilly bonnet. We do have very deep roots in our community.

Our fathers played on the same football team at Luverne High School. We have the picture to prove that connection.

Mamaw loved snake stories. She saved them up to share with me. Sometimes I would beg her to retell some of the best.

She told about a tenant farmer on the old Odom's Bridge Road, which is now our Airport Road. She said that man was walking to the house after a full day's work in the fields. He saw something out of the corner of his eye and when a huge rattlesnake struck at him, he caught it in this hands. The story goes that the snake started spewing venom in the farmer's face. He stayed sick for several days just due to contact with the snake's venom.

An old farmer had all the symptoms of being bitten on the foot by a poisonous snake. He had much swelling of his foot and his leg and finally died. No one could find the snake and didn't even understand how the encounter happened. When his widow was cleaning out his belongings after his death, she gave one of the farm hands his favorite boots. The hand couldn't wait to wear the boots, but when he put them on, he felt a prick and the snake fang was buried in the bottom of the boot and the story goes that he died soon after.

A humorous story was that the matriarch of the family attended the family reunion. After a big meal, she went to the outhouse. The family heard her scream and went rushing to the back yard. The crowd got there just in time to see her leave the outhouse with her skirt around her head and her panties around her ankles. She was screaming "Snake, snake.´ There was a huge chicken snake in the rafters and it had dropped down at face level. The snake was killed, but she never got her pride back.

There was a Luverne businessman who was deathly afraid of snakes. The rascally children hid in the bushes by the sidewalk. As the man walked home from his work about sundown, the kids drug a stuffed stocking in the front of the man by a long string. The string wrapped around the man's ankle and followed him all the way home. My grandmother said the man had a convulsion that night and that all the kids who were involved got serious belt whippings.

There was a County Pond tale. A rather rotund woman was fishing with her husband. They fished from the bank. As they packed up to leave about dark, a big mocassin struck at the lady. The snake missed by a few centimeters. Its fangs became tangled in the woman's drawers and she ran, but couldn't lose the snake. She was not injured, but it was told that she ran until the snakes' fangs tore through the cotton and fell to the ground. The word was that the woman never cared to go back fishing.

In the spring, Mamaw went fishing every day that it wasn't raining. She saw snakes nearly everyday. She normally didn't kill non-poisonous snakes, but she really wanted to get rid of the mocassins. Daddy gave her a sawed-off shotgun for Mother's Day. She loved her gift and cleared out lots of dangerous snakes. She was in her late 70's when she got that special gift.

Once a bird had built a little nest in the fireplace at Mamaw's when she was a very young woman. When some of her little nieces and nephews visited, she told them to go look at the pretty bird eggs. They came back in the room where she was and had such strange looks on their faces. She went to check on the bird eggs. They had been eaten by a huge chicken snake that was curled up on top of the nest. Mamaw told this story for years.

When my grandparents moved to town in the early 70's, Mamaw told me that she really missed the wildlife on the farm. She said I really want to see one more "good" snake before I die. I thought that was a strange comment, but I understand it much better now. A few days after she made this statement, a huge rattlesnake was coiled under her carport in the middle of Luverne. She called Daddy to bring his gun and come kill the snake. She spent about an hour looking at it. She watched it wiggle and squirm in the strange death throes that snakes have. An old saying was that a snake wouldn't stop wiggling until the sun went down. Mamaw was very happy with how her day turned out and she had a smile on her face all that day.

I come from strange people. Before Billy married me, he claims that he drove up to the farm and observed Mamaw pull a six foot long chicken snake from a tree in the pasture. He married me anyway. We aren't boring.

****

I am not writing about undergarments today. I'm going for something far more annoying. I looked for a picture of a red physical education romper, but decided this is close enough. Horrible! Janice Williamson Roberts' post about not having the privilege of wearing pants to school made me think of this monstrosity. The very worst part of moving up to the high school in the 60s. And we wore these in the gym which we shared with the boys. The guys were running around half naked and the girls were attired in these.

The red was a dull maroon and not even close to Luverne red. The best thing about this memory is that it is way in the past. Now I see that rompers are currently in style for men. Are you kidding me? Welcome to it, fellows! Been there, done that!

****

A talk about classmate Lewis Jones that I partially delivered to a Class of '65 Reunion:

Lewis Jones (L.J.)

The first story I could collect about Lewis Jones was that Mike Jones....no relation....told me he met Lewis for the first time when he broke up a fight in a back alley in Luverne between Lewis and Richard Sport....According to Mike... it was over a girl. Since Richard is not here...I can say that I imagine Mike saved Richard from a real ass whuppin'.

Lewis came to LHS in the ninth grade from Capital Heights in Montgomery. To us he was a sophisticated city boy with hygiene standards far beyond most of you country boys. He was always slicked up and he smelled great....all the time.

When Lewis moved to Petrey he had recently broken his hand badly pole vaulting and had metal pins in the back of his hand. That gave some of us an excuse to look at his scars and secretly hold his hand in class....which was major romance in the early sixties.

Lewis was a renowned flirt. At his funeral his sister-in-law told me that he was a flirt to the very end. She said that he was propositioning the nurses at the hospital and attempting to lure them into his bed as he was dying. Somehow that personally comforts me.

I know that Lewis loved his car. He enjoyed shining up his '52 Chevy. He constantly worked on it and hated ever getting off the pavement and riding the dirt roads. He was the original bad boy before we ever heard of Grease and the T-Birds....before John Travolta and Patrick Swayze made that sort of character intriguing.

Friends say that Lewis worked extremely hard to maintain his bad ass reputation. He loved being cocky and arrogant. He has even been described as uppity. People who really knew him said that he took after his mother who was more refined and fastidious....a little above it all. His Daddy was described as a common, ordinary salt of the Earth southern man. That Lewis was not!

Lewis played a little football in the 11th grade mainly because Mike did, but he became a good ball player as a senior.... A starter. But basically Lewis found his greatest joy in pissing people off on a regular basis. Over the years he got real good at it.

Surprisingly I found out that every year at Christmas, Lewis would contribute to local churches for their programs to help underprivileged children....I don't mean a couple of churches...I am talking 8-10 churches. He never wanted any of his good deeds known because he had worked too hard to establish his rebellious, bad-boy reputation.

Lewis loved children...even though he never had any of his own. He liked giving things to kids and being around kids and he was truthfully a man with a kind heart and a soft spot for children.

I got to know Lewis all over again when he ran the service station in town. He took care of me and my car. He was genuinely interested in my family and especially my children. He was actually a pretty sweet guy in his middle age.

Lewis did have his problems. Life boils down to two types of folks....those who we wonder what their vices are and those we KNOW about. Lewis didn't have too many secrets here in town. The comment was made that Lewis was too proud to get help when he really needed it. His last couple of months were really, really rough. He died in a Veterans facility in August of 2008.

Lewis did serve three years in Vietnam. He volunteered for additional tours of duty there. For that I think many of us who didn't go, who got by without having a husband or a family member go....well, we owe Lewis a debt for his patriotism.

In fact....more than likely...this song written in the 60's was for the L.J.s of this world.

Life is ... Common Ground

He's a rebel and he'll never be any good.

He's a rebel and he never ever does what he should.

And just because he doesn't do what everybody else does

That's no reason why we can't give him all our love.

In spite of yourself…The Class of '65 does love you…Lewis Jones!

****

Motherless Child

In the early fall of 1958, I was 11 and in the 6th grade at Luverne Elementary. My teacher was Ms. Gladys Hicks. I got off to a strange start this school year. We lived in the Bricken House on Third Street. I had the back bedroom that was very much like a private suite. I was the only girl and the oldest, but we had a sweet, little cousin come into our lives for a few months. We were accustomed to many cousins on the Folmar side, but this child was our kin on the Perdue side. She lived in Montgomery with her parents. She was an only child. Her Daddy was in the Hiway Patrol and was an officer or in administration. We now call that group State Troopers. Her mother was Betty Lane Perdue Bishop. She was one of the most beautiful women in our family.

She looked so much like the movie stars in my Aunt's movie magazines. Our Aunt, Daddy's sister, Judy Perdue worked at the Archives and History Building. In our minds, she ran the place. She even had her own parking spot right at the back door. She was close with her cousin, Betty Lane, probably because they both lived in the city. Betty Lane had dark, thick black hair. She wore it in a bob and the edges curled around her face. She had a fabulous figure and she wore dark red lipstick. She was very glamorous and poised. Her brother was a doctor. He lived in Louisiana, but he had come to Luverne to take care of his beautiful sister. After I was an adult I found out that she had very invasive breast cancer and was at the end of her fight. She had several relatives in Luverne and she had many friends. In truth, she had come home to die. I don't think we had ever been told this, but we lived for

93

several weeks where the family members talked in whispers and I seldom heard any laughter. Very unusual for fun loving jokesters, who always had the volume at full blast. I was a kid, but I knew that serious things were happening.

Daddy was very close to his first cousin, Dr. Mervin Perdue. They looked a lot alike. They were both dark, handsome, Southern gentlemen. They hunted and fished and bonded as many men do through all their hobbies. Daddy was very proud of all Dr. Perdue had accomplished, but when they got together they seemed like boys to me, clowning around, cracking jokes. All the happy had gone at this point.

Bonnie hung out with me as the summer slipped away. Mama had fixed her a little cot in our playroom, but she mostly slept with me. School started and I think I remember that Bonnie even went to school in Luverne for a few days all along. I think the school allowed this for a short while. It was not unusual for visitors or relatives from out of town to hang out at school with the registered students.

Bonnie had been to the hospital to visit her mother for a little while. She came back to spend the night at the Bricken house with us. Her father and her uncle were at the hospital with her sick mother. She had a little trouble drifting off to sleep. I came in and slipped into bed with her. She went on to sleep cuddled up against me. I think I finally went to sleep and didn't bother to go back to my bedroom.

I heard the telephone ring in the middle of the night. A late night phone call was nearly always bad news. Very seldom would anyone disturb a family this late. I could tell that it was bad. The call was from Dr. Perdue and he had called Daddy to tell him that beautiful Betty Lane had died at 33 years of age. I could hear Mama and Daddy talking softly. I heard Daddy start to cry. This had never happened before. I had never seen my Daddy cry. It terrified me. The fact that a seven year old could lose her mother terrified me. Daddy dressed and as he was leaving for the hospital, he stuck his head in to check on Bonnie. She was sound asleep in her little girl pajamas. Daddy brushed her hair back from her face. He told me, "Go back to sleep. There is nothing you can do. Don't tell Bonnie a thing if she wakes up." I put my arms around Bonnie and I felt the tears slip down my cheeks. I didn't understand how this could happen.

The next time I saw her was several weeks after the funeral. She looked like a normal kid to me. Her father had business in Montgomery and he left Bonnie for the weekend. It stuck in my mind that before he left he made her wear socks with flip flops. We were having one of those warm spells that sometimes happen in the South, even if it was the middle of winter. That night he called long distance to make sure that she was okay and then he called two more times. He had become so very over-protective. I felt so sorry for her because I knew she wouldn't be able to have the carefree life she would have enjoyed if she had still had her mother. I visited her a few times in Montgomery. And then the families drifted apart and we lost touch.

****

The Interview with Bridget

I was born in 1947. I am 70 years old. I will start on your question #5, but will say a few things about World War II.

I grew up hearing about the attack on Pearl Harbor. It stunned Americans. Both my parents served in the military. My Dad was a Merchant Marine and my Mom was in the Navy. Females were in the WAVES. They married after the war in 1946 and I was born 11 months later.

The Korean War started when I was 3 and ended when I was 6. I remembered some horrible stories of that war and some of the local men who fought in it that were a little younger than my Dad. War was a scary word to most kids. There were Veterans in nearly every community who had PTSD, which was then called being "shell shocked". They would sometimes have spells from noises and also were often talking to themselves. Most people had sympathy and understanding for them. When I was a child, our community was very patriotic. The flag was almost sacred to adults and children.

The Cold War went on when I was in elementary and Junior High. We considered Russia/USSR as a scary enemy, but there was no real fighting between the U.S. and Russia. There seemed to be constant threats and nuclear tests. Both sides stockpiled nuclear arsenals. I remember children having dog tags for identification. We also practiced drills for a nuclear war like we do fire drills now. It was constantly on our minds that something big and bad might happen.

During the Cuban Missile Crisis in 1962 we had a fall-out shelter in our basement. We had supplies of food and water. My parents were very serious about it. I was about Junior High age when this went on. Daddy kept a gun because he said that when people got hungry that they might come to steal our supplies.

I also remember in high school that we took a class on first aid and on how to survive a nuclear attack. We were taught how to deliver a baby. That was a big deal back in the 60s. We giggled and blushed during this class, but it was very frightening to us.

Eisenhower was an Army general and a Republican. He was president from the time I was about 6 until I was a teenager. Back then we respected the President, whoever they were. Being a general in the military earned lots of admiration with the American public. Ike and his wife, Mamie, seemed very old to me. Richard Nixon was the Vice President. I remember Eisenhower as being a peace maker and trying to ease the tensions of the Cold War.

My husband and I graduated from Luverne High in 1965. We were friends, but did not date in high school. I remember the day that JFK was assassinated. I was standing right outside the gym door. When I was told that the President was dead, it really didn't upset me to start with. In general the Kennedys were hated in the South and viewed as rich snobs. Within a few days, I realized that losing our American President was a big deal. When I watched his family on TV, I began to feel sorry for them.

My class was the last segregated class at Luverne. There were several other white graduation classes, but there was also black students at the school in the late 60s. I had grown up with black women who worked as cooks and housekeepers for my family. My family loved these ladies and we were not allowed to ever use the "N" word. There were plenty of people around who claimed to hate black people. My granddaddy told me once that in the South we might claim to hate the race, but we loved the individuals. I get that now because the blacks who work around whites got to know each other and they just became people.

When I went to college in Birmingham, I had black people in my nursing school. I also took care of black patients. I quickly got used to living in an integrated world.

The Vietnam War was a horrible cloud hanging over the families that I knew. My husband and I married in 1968. He was a senior at Troy State University. We were so worried that he would be sent to Vietnam after he graduated from college. The strangest thing kept him at home. He had a terrible skin condition called eczema. It caused him to fail his physical. They did not draft him because of the possibility of him getting an infection and being on military disability for the rest of his life. One of my brothers got in the National Guard and another was at risk of a lottery that went by the birthdays of the boys. He was far enough down the list that we didn't think he would have to serve. I had many, many relatives and friends who went to Vietnam. It was a war that seemed to go on and on. There were so many pictures of flag draped coffins being brought home to the States. That was a horrible way to live back then.

****

Elmwood Cemetery in Birmingham, Alabama, is huge. It covers over 400 acres. Bear Bryant is buried there. So are many of my family members on Mama's side of the family.

When I went up to handle some school business in 1965, before I moved to Birmingham to start nursing school, I visited Elmwood with my Grandmother Williams. It was impossible to locate my Granddaddy's grave without her. Elmwood was a virtual maze. I had purchased a few gladiolus to leave on his grave. Grandmother easily directed me to Pawpaw's resting place. We had a quiet moment. There was not much to see or say. He had died young, in his sleep, in his bed with his wife. I remember being stunned when Mama got the call. I hadn't seen many tears from Mama. When she did cry, it was from frustration and exhaustion. Usually when we broke something or bled on a new outfit or lost a good pair of shoes. Grief looked and sounded very different. She went to Birmingham alone. Daddy probably had to work, to make payroll, to keep up with us.

Anyway.... a dozen years later, I paid my respects. When I started to leave the glads, Grandmother said "Let's take those pretty flowers back to the house. We can enjoy them all weekend. They'll just wilt here." This little story just might explain a few things about why I'm the way I am. Live for the moment. Rest in peace, Pawpaw and Grandmother Williams.

****

Ritz-Carlton, Naples, Florida. Yes, Pat and Billy actually vacationed here several times back in the day. Billy's little trucking company was going strong and he was a member of Florida Feed Association. The annual meetings were held at beautiful locations throughout the State. This morning when I was unpacking from our Easter trip to Lake Martin, I suddenly vividly recalled our check-in at the Ritz. Clueless bumpkins, no doubt. We drove over 500 miles from Luverne, Alabama to South Florida in our raggedy old van. We didn't fly. Still don't. At that time, I don't think we owned real luggage. We did have several Piggly Wiggly bags. Pretty sure we had flip flops, sun hats, and beach towels scattered all over our car. Really all that was missing was the theme song from Beverly Hillbillys.

As a bellman was escorting us to our stunning beachside room, he mentioned to Billy that a tie and dinner jacket was a necessity for one of their very upscale restaurants. I'm pretty certain that he knew there was no dinner jacket crammed into one of those brown bags. Billy did tip the poor fellow extravagantly. We had a fun time even though we were very much out of our comfort zone. You can take us out of the country, but you can't take the country out of Pat and Billy.

****

Life is ... Common Ground

This is not a joke, but it made me smile when our cousin posted it. Oakland Memorial Gardens. Mama Mary's older sister, Ella Beatrice Williams, who died as a toddler, is buried here. She lies in an overgrown area known as the old church section. When Mama got old and rambled some in her thoughts, she told me this child died in the night in the bed with her. I never knew if that was true or if Mama's brain was playing tricks on her. I loved her two sisters and two brothers so much. Hard to imagine there was a sixth sibling that died so young and was never a part of our lives.

Family is family. I prefer to think of her as an adult aunt who is drinking coffee and laughing with her brothers and sisters in Heaven. Who knows? Little Beatrice could be the Guardian Angel that got this group of wild Perdues through many close calls, high fevers, and allergies to bees and wasps. We will just keep you, little lost girl, in the OMG cemetery.

****

When it finally stopped raining, I just happened to notice some worm damage in a catawba tree. The sight brought back lots of fishing memories.
Spelled several different ways, Catawba worms were what Mamaw called them. These fat things are the grossest fish bait ever. Mamaw had a big cage she kept them in. She also had a small portable cage that she used to carry them to the fish pond. I helped her gather them. We would keep a sharp eye out for catawba trees that had evidence of leaves that had been eaten away. We used

an extra long bamboo pole to slap the branches in the tree and dislodge the bait. I have had worms land in my hair, on my face, and once down my blouse. These things have a nasty habit of spitting slime when they are disturbed. Gathering catawba worms is a nasty business, but fish do love the worms. They spit when you put them on your fish hook. I have caught some mighty fine bream with catawba bait. My granddaddy called the thick, colorful bream stump knockers. After cleaning up from handling bait, cleaning fish, and disposing of fish innards, I have enjoyed many a family fish fry. When we had fish, we had fish. No trimmings needed. We used the grab it and growl approach. As soon as the fish were cool enough to hold, we ate right out of the brown paper bags they were dumped into. We always ate the crispy backfin. Might have been the best part. As soon as we were weaned, we were old enough to "look out for the bones". I wouldn't take a thing for my raising. Those were the days. If you're not Southern, you might not understand being nostalgic for slime spitting fishbait and your grandmaw.

****

My grandmother was not perfect!

My Mother's Mother was a strong Christian woman. She was not as much fun as my country grandmother, but she was pretty great. Her church was her life. She attended Parkview Baptist Church all the years that I knew her. She went to most activities that the church scheduled. Grandmother Williams was pretty strict and had very high moral standards. But she had a flaw.

It took me years to figure it out. Grandmother had a particular smell that I had smelled on some of the country women in Crenshaw County. At first I just couldn't identify it. Also Grandmother had an odd behavior. She would wander along the side walk that went around her block. Sometimes she would step into the gutter or the edge of the quiet neighborhood street. I would peep out the window in the living room and try to figure out just what she was doing. Finally one day I saw her picking up an old cigarette. It hit me. The odor was tobacco and my sweet, rigid Grandmother was scavenging for tossed, previously smoked cigarettes. She'd unroll the cigarette and take out the tobacco and put it in her mouth. It seemed so gross to me and this was before the days of AIDS and other terrifying communicable diseases. I can only assume she did this for years.

When she got older and less stable on her feet, her daughter in law, who had apparently watched her for years, did the sweetest thing. She bought cigarettes for her teenage son, who may or may not have smoked, and made these cigarettes available to Grandmother. My cousin spent most of his nights with our grandmother. It was all on the sly, but Grandmother was able to have her cigarettes and keep her dignity. She would never have consented to buying herself tobacco, snuff, or chewing tobacco. I respected and loved my aunt and my grandmother more than ever. I say that Yes, you can measure love.

****

I very seldom sleep late, but I did. Promised a story inspired by the handsome guy at Bass Pro who carried a huge bow. Luverne High School physical education department decided to branch into uncharted territory and teach the big kids archery. Very few of us were good at it. I do think this particular incident occurred after I got my first pair of glasses from Dr. Watson. Prior to the glasses, I couldn't have seen the target or the hay bales that supported it. Truth be known, I bumped one of my Granddaddy's calves in his pasture as I was learning to drive. I was not being reckless, I was blind.

As we were "learning" archery, I was interested in wearing the protective gear that prevented one from peeling off a layer of skin when you loaded the bow and released the arrow. I remember we got 3 arrows, 3 tries. My first two arrows were flops. One didn't even make it to the target and the second one grazed the edge of the hay bale supporting the target.

On my last try, I pulled back on the bow and let my arrow fly. Apparently I had found some hidden strength, but not a dab of accuracy. My arrow took flight, above the hay bales, the target, and over the top of the bleachers. I screamed as only a teenage southern girl can. I ran around the bleachers and onto the football field. In the center of the field was a boy with the arrow protruding from his chest. That brought screaming to a whole new level. I want to think the wounded guy was Charles West. I'm sure he won't remember. It was a joke! A big, not funny joke!

Anyway the victim had grabbed up the arrow from the grass, where it had harmlessly fallen and stuck it under his arm. It looked just like he had been shot when he stretched out on the 50 yard line and successfully looked dead. The guys in the PE class howled and hooted. It took my teenaged heart a long time to return to normal rhythm. I did not wish to graduate as Most Likely to Kill a Classmate. I think that was pretty much the end of archery at LHS. Or at least for that school year. Who would ever have thought that I would have gone on to teach high school students for over 25 years.....but I didn't teach archery.

****

Guy L Perdue

Daddy was the fun parent. Mama was the disciplinarian.Daddy was somewhat like an older teenage brother. Mama was in charge. I respected Daddy, but I was afraid of Mama.

Daddy and Mama were married 11 months before I arrived. I was not ever an easy baby or a relaxed toddler. Mama decided she was way smarter than Daddy, but he was a good business man and used his considerable charm when he needed it. We had happy childhoods. I was a young wife with a baby when their marriage fell apart.

Early on I remember spreading quilts on the floor and listening to Amos and Andy with Daddy. He would pop corn and we would eat out of the individual silver plate baby cups that were the traditional baby gift back in the day. Daddy kept strange foods around that we ate because he ate them.....sardines, ripe bananas, raw oatmeal, prune juice. We thought those were treats. Daddy put us to bed with Froggy Went a Courtin' and the Robin Hood songs. Also remember hush little baby.

Daddy was a fitness nut before it was the thing. He lifted weights and jumped rope. I often fell asleep to the sounds of Daddy working out. He also ran wearing combat boots. Guy Perdue was very handsome, fit, and brown. Mama was the exact opposite with very white skin and she was so skinny that her legs did not touch when she put them together. Daddy kept this picture and showed it to us often of our skinny mother.

We often enjoyed homemade ice cream from a churn that Daddy turned. In the fall Daddy brought home sugar cane. He peeled it from the top, meaning that we chewed the fairly tasteless top part before we got to the sweet part at the bottom of the stalk. Daddy loved to buy cane juice from an old farmer who used a horse to mash the stalks and sold the juice in old liquor bottles. It never tasted as good as the juice we chewed out of the bottom of a stalk. The process of eating the cane was sacred. Daddy split each piece into four section and we each had a bite of each level. Everything was all equal for the Perdues. We got equal sections of watermelon. Mama counted the oysters and we each got exact equal numbers of fried oysters. She even counted the meatballs in Chef Boyardee canned spaghetti. There were six little meatballs with some meat and lots of filler. 1 1/2 meatballs for each Perdue.

When we had camp stew in the fall, we were served the stew on a single slice of white bread. The stew was divided into six equal servings. That may be why I love stew so much as an old lady. Camp Stew was a fund raiser item and we ate a lot of it in the fall and winter.

When Daddy grilled steaks, he did not believe in using charcoal. Our job would be to pick up little sticks and limbs from the yard. Daddy would use those and let them burn down for a fire. His grilling was perfection and it would be done his way.

In my mind, we had a happy, fun, secure childhood. That all changed later, but I wouldn't change a thing. I think younger days are more important than teen years. There is so much drama and angst during the high school years. We just didn't have to manufacture our drama, it found us. That will be another long story.

Life is... Family!

My favorite Perdue kid game was Tarzan when we were kids and lived in the Bricken House on First Street in town. We had a great back yard that extended into woods that went all the way to the river. We had plenty of thick vines and trees to climb. Cast of characters: Bob was Tarzan, big, strong, silent. I was Jane, glamorous and, well, the only female.. Jim was Boy, spokesperson for the family,smart and well educated and of course, Tom was Cheetah, nuf said. Perfect. I remember posting this several years ago, but it needs repeating.

"Pat at 14 months" was scribbled on the back of this picture of me. This was made about a year before Bob was born. Then he was quickly followed by Jim and Tom. Somehow Mama Mary had a miscarriage in the midst of all this. Five pregnancies in a mere seven years.

Until I found this pic, I never realized I had ever worn a hair bow. At one point, Mama actually tried with me. I guess she eventually gave up. I was just fine with three younger brothers. Suddenly I am nearly 70, known as the Life is Good lady. I love family, flowers, football, and food.

Glad there is photographic proof that I once had some frou frou in my life. Thank you, Mama.

****

This morning I'm having my own little Homecoming experience with my great memories and my second cup of coffee. One wonderful thing about retirement is time.....quiet time, time to reflect, time without one eye on the clock. This is something that would be wasted on the young. Also it's good to be a little bit lazy and enjoy sitting.

Life is... Family!

Mama charmingly called these Pat's rat's nests. I loved stringing blankets and sheets from couch to chair to coffee table. Old quilts would pad the inside. I required a light source because I'd cuddle in and read once my project was complete. Mama would complain because her neat house was destroyed. I promised to straighten up when I was done, but that never fully happened.

Now I'm retired with my own little space. Billy laughed this morning as I made my nest and settled in the living room. My new electric firelogs were instantly burning by the magic of remote control. The front door was opened so I could watch the birds feed on the scattered seed. I have pansies that Donny Ray Holmes planted in pots with still frozen soil. My smell-good contraption is lit and aroma therapy was doing its job. Hot coffee from the Keurig was poured into my brand new Life is Good mug. My arthritis bean bag hot packs were warm and toasty from the microwave. I'm wearing fuzzy socks with imbeded aloe and wrapped in a soft blanket. Some habits never change. Aren't we glad?

Life is ... Common Ground

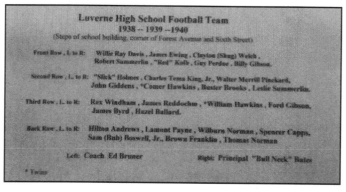

Luverne High School Football Team
1938 -- 1939 --1940
(Steps of school building, corner of Forest Avenue and Sixth Street)

Front Row , L to R: Willie Ray Davis , James Ewing , Clayton (Slug) Welch ,
Robert Summerlin , "Red" Kolb , Guy Perdue , Billy Gibson.

Second Row , L to R: "Slick" Holmes , Charles Tema King, Jr., Walter Merrill Pinckard,
John Giddens , *Comer Hawkins , Buster Brooks , Leslie Summerlin.

Third Row , L. to R: Rex Windham , James Reddoch , *William Hawkins , Ford Gibson,
James Byrd , Hazel Ballard.

Back Row , L. to R: Hilton Andrews , Lamont Payne , Wilburn Norman , Spencer Capps,
Sam (Bub) Boswell, Jr., Brown Franklin , Thomas Norman

Left: Coach Ed Bruner   Right: Principal "Bull Neck" Bates

* Twins

Our only grandson, William Patrick Davis, enters Luverne High
School in a few days. A long family tradition and deep roots
continue. Two of his great grandfathers played together on this
Tiger Team in the late 1930s. Front row: Willie Ray Davis #9 and
Guy Perdue #60. Go Big Red!

* *

I woke up thinking about Luverne football and how I've always
loved it. Daddy had an old Jeep that looked like a box on wheels.
It had no seats in the back. One afternoon I just happened to be
hanging around the gym when football practice ended. In the

107

60s, very few teenagers had their own cars. I was lucky to get to use the Jeep. That day several guys asked me to take them home. Exactly how I hoped things would work out. I remember three of these fellows...... Charles West, Morris Tate, and Poodlum Davis. I knew it was a little bit beyond the city limit sign. My parents told me not to go beyond those boundaries without permission. I was too thrilled to have a Jeep full of sweaty, smelly Tigers to bother with that little technicality. No calamities occurred, even though Poodlum lived on a dirt road on the back side of nowhere. I was home before dark and even set the table for supper. When the six of us were seated and after the blessing, Mama casually asked, "What did you do after school?" I said I went by the dime store for a piece of poster paper and I went back to school to get a textbook I forgot. And what else Mama asked. I gave somebody a ride after football practice. Mama and Daddy kept staring at me. Daddy took over then. You've been to Glenwood, right? You do know that lying by omission is still lying, right? You are grounded. No more taxi service for Tigers after football practice. You'll be riding with your Mama and your brothers to and from school for a month. Yes, Sir. I answered. My eyes teared up and I asked to be excused. I noticed all three of my brothers were smirking as I went to my bedroom. I really wasn't sorry. I was just sorry I got caught. Hauling Tigers that chilly afternoon was so worth it. I noticed they didn't ban me from the Friday night game. Here I sit. 70 years old and still a LHS Tiger fan. And I have my memories.

****

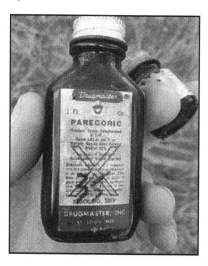

When we coughed at our granddaddy's, Virgil G. Perdue, would give us a spoon full of sugar with Paregoric drizzled on it. Opium that could be purchased until the 1970s, without a prescription. I do remember sleeping really well in an unheated bedroom, under a mountain of quilts.

****

I absolutely do not understand why I am hung up on stories of undergarments, but here we go again. In the late 50's these starched petticoats were the thing. All the girls had them. They were the epitome of style. The girls on American Bandstand twirled in them on television. The big problem for me was that Mama made it my job to starch my own petticoats. She pretty well had her parenting priorities in order. Every Saturday morning I would wash the netting, make up the liquid starch solution, and dip the limp fabric into a big dishpan of the goo. What price beauty! I would clip the edge of the garment with clothespins and hang the completed project on the clothes line to dry in a big white circle. Not one of my three brothers ever messed with my petticoats. They knew it was too risky to go there. Perdue boys had their limits.

On Monday mornings the petticoat would lift my skirts out like a square dance partner There was a scratch factor. My legs often looked like I had waltzed through a briar patch. By Friday the thing would be limp and sagging. I don't remember a single girl who owned more than one petticoat.

One day at play period I went down the old metal slide on the playground at Luverne Elementary School. The bottom row of petticoat netting snagged on the metal frame at the top of the slide. I can still hear the sound of fabric tearing as I made the trip all the way down the slide. My teacher helped me gather all the starched netting in my arms. I went to the Girls Restroom and removed the whole contraption. The janitor gave me a paper bag to hold all that netting. I remember rushing back out to play. I was not one bit embarrassed or shy. Mamaw sewed it all back together on her Singer sewing machine with the foot pedal. I wore that ridiculous thing for the rest of the school year. I smile now as I see the holey jeans and the cutout shoulders on the girls when the school dismissal bell rings. We were the queens of style back in our day. You've got nothing on me.

Life is Will

"Willisms"

My grandson has been on a wonderful trip with the other side of the family. Been gone for over a week. When I walked into his house, this child smiled and said to me, "Hey, Ya Ya! Let the spoiling begin!"

Only man on this planet who totally has my number. I would not change a thing.

Will: Ya Ya, I will give up video games next year for Lent if you will give up Facebook.

Me: Will, when you get 70 it is not about giving up things. It's about what you can keep. I'm not giving up Facebook until I die and go to Heaven, Hell, or wherever. They won't have Facebook there.

Will: I know. They don't have a good website.

I wet my pants.

A Will funny. He might be cutting back on junk. Just gave him $20 in a Halloween card. He told me he was putting it in a college fun. He quipped, I meant to say fun, not fund. I am planning on having some fun when I get to college.

I have a funny grandchild. This morning three babies were on the Today Show and were in little chairs that rocked, bounced and jiggled the babes. Will looked at me and said, "Hmmmm! Pretty soon they won't even need grandmas any more!"

He gave me a big grin and we both laughed. I feel safe in my role.

Life is Will

I love that Facebook reminds us of things we posted in years past. I love funny kid stories. Will was 9 years old when he made Ya Ya laugh out loud.

"This morning when a motorcycle went down Airport Road, I commented to my grandson that I was glad I didn't have to ride a motorcycle to work on this chilly morning. Will said, "This is pretty much your job right here. You don't have to ride anywhere!" Glad I have a JOB that I love."

Wes told Will yesterday. Until you are 40, you have to respect everybody. After 40 you don't have to respect everybody. After 60 you don't have to respect anybody.

Home from our latest beach adventure. Back to the routine. Took Will to school. When we asked him where we drop off a 7th grader, he replied, "I'll tell you when we get there, I don't want to confuse you."

Coffee makes everything better, but a grandson for breakfast makes life great! He informed me that the nice thing about old women is that they are good cooks. I will accept any compliment I receive from this child.

We eat our pizza and Will has a fit about the anchovies. He says, "Trust me, Ya-Ya. Don't eat that fish." We laugh, but we both love anchovies on pizza. On the way out Billy and Will waste several quarters in some silly candy machines.

Later Will gets frustrated and fires us both on the way home. He says that we are too old, too slow when we do things, and not cool. He is pretty accurate with that. He finally rehires Billy and agrees to let me come to his Tee-Ball game tonight.

Will calls the elevator in the Courthouse the up-down.

Cute thing. Will plays in an inflatable raft at the Lake. Two seven-year-old boys brag that they are big enough to ride a tube with nobody with them. Wes says that he rides with "yes body". Too funny.

Turning Thirteen

It hit me that Will is turning 13 this year. I so clearly remember hanging that bouquet of blue balloons on the post by my entryway to the basement at Luverne High School.

Will has an old soul. He gets adult humor and subtlety. I think even more than Julie did. He is so comfortable in our adult world.

Funny tale. On the way home from Atlanta, I ate too richly at Steak and Shake. Naturally we had to hunt a service station on Pike Road and I had to make two runs inside. Of course, Billy with an old man's prostate, has to get out and check the tires every 30 minutes. When we finally got south of Montgomery, Billy eased down a dirt road. Will slipped his earphones off that burr head and asked "Peeing or Pooping?"

Like Grandma, Like Grandson

I wish I could have recorded Will this afternoon. So aware of politics and current events. Deep thinker. Then he went in post office and told me it was locked down. I fell for it and he burst out laughing. He said "Ya Ya, You are just too easy."

I enjoy every minute we have. Today he said something close to....."Like Grandma,.Like Grandson." I almost cried.

Will & YaYa

Thank you, Facebook Friends, for hanging in there with me through my excessive celebration of Will's birthday week. I figure that the general response may be #1 Thank goodness she only has one grandchild. #2 Wish she had several grandchildren so she could spread it out a little bit. Or #3 How does that unfollow or delete deal work?

This was bound to happen. It is in my DNA. I had two wonderfully affectionate grandmothers. They were both full of crazy love for their grandchildren. My grandmothers were so perfect that I often thought of running away from home and going to live with a grandmother.

Actually, I did run away once to live with Mamaw. The problem with this escape attempt was that I was a poor speller. I had to ask my mother how to spell so many of the words in my good bye note that she pretty early on figured out my plan. She told me to go clean up my room and not to dare step outside of the house.

It ended up that at that very time, a night fisherman on the Patsaliga was attacked by a rabid fox, just a few hundred yards from our back door. I always thought that being a poor speller probably saved my life. Obviously I was the dramatic Perdue child.

Best Laid Plans

March 12, 2010

"the best laid plans of mice and men" and grandmothers.

You will just have to bear with me for this tale. It may take a while.

The first day of school I took Will to registration because Wes had to drive a bus and Ashley had a meeting. The teacher was assigning dates for Friday Surprise. These are treats for children who have behaved all week, but I think that most students do end up getting a Friday Surprise. I made certain to put down Will's name for (March 12) this particular day because his birthday always seems to fall during Spring Break. Miss Sandy (Will's other grandmother---Mrs. Pat Walker) planned to do cupcakes and I was to do other treats. This was a sneaky way to have a quasi-birthday party in a school that does not allow birthday parties. Please note that this was planned last August.

Turns out today was the big reading day for the elementary school. I ordered Will a tee shirt from the school....all the better for photo opportunities. The featured book was Where The Wild Things Are. There was a little wild thing on every cupcake. I was loaded down with other little treats. Everything is going according to plans.

Wes calls as I am driving to school. Will is in the nurse's office threatening to throw up. Wes, Ashley and I arrive at the school at the exact same moment. Will feels too bad to even go back to his classroom. We bless the other children with the treats while Will sits in the truck with his Dad. He did manage to pass a tremendous amount of intestinal gas while waiting for us to distribute the goodies. Somehow the males in my family found this to be extremely humorous.

The good news is that Dr. Pat checked Will out and he seems to be fine. Will and Ashley are now at the beach for several days of spring break. Somehow my visions of sweet photos and boisterous first graders singing Happy Birthday just went by the wayside. I have enclosed a photo of the cupcakes and the book. Just imagine Will in the picture.

I should have written for the Carol Burnette Show. I seem to be living it. If you want to hear God laugh....make a plan.

"Don't let that child watch too much TV and play those video games. He'll never care about reading and his grades will plummet."

So far, so good.

A Will Story

A couple of weekends ago, Will was working on a Habitat for Humanity project. One of the volunteers told Ashley that Will was over behind a dumpster. She went to check on him, thinking he was sick or upset. Oh, no. Will asked her if she noticed the guy with the clipboard. He thought it was an OSHA inspector and he knew kids were supposed to be 16 to be legal. Ashley told him that the clipboard guy was a preacher, not an inspector. Billy loved this tale. Wes had to dodge the law when he worked at Harbin Freight and our trucking business. I guess Will has actually listened to some of the old family stories.

Battle with a Baby

I decide to go with Julie and Wes to a Home Depot in Atlanta. I hope that Will is going to nap in the truck. Big mistake. It takes the kids over an hour in Home Depot. I am doing the best that I can with Will, but he is all over the place. He is cute when he loves on his imaginary dog and then calls my imaginary dog in Luverne and has him drive to Atlanta in his tiny imaginary car. He does the same thing with our imaginary E.T.s and somehow he acquires an additional E.T. He begins to wear down and gets so ready to go home.

Will goes totally wild when I get a phone call. Ends up he tries to crawl up on the dash and breaks off a CD in Billy's player. I cannot get part of the CD out and the machine is making terrible noises. I don't want Wes to have to worry about this and I don't want Billy to get mad.

Will knows that I am angry. He can't get the words out, but he asks, " You mean, Ya-Ya?" He starts ranting that he is going to walk to his mother's and that he won't play with me anymore. I almost call the kids, but they finally come outside.

We stop to gas up. I pay to fill up Billy's truck. I go inside the QT to buy some diet cokes and other supplies. I hunt for sweet tea for Will because he has finished off all his Ya-Ya juice. When I come out I find out that the broken CD ejected when Wes cranked the truck and everyone is relieved. We go home and Julie orders Chinese.

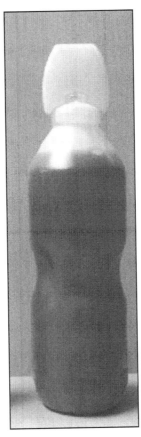

Ya Ya Juice

Valentine's Day- Will is Three

We start right in playing the Computer fish game. I coax Will into clothes and finally we leave around 11:30. He is so funny when I add a cute plaid flannel shirt on top of his white t-shirt. "Ya-Ya, two shirts?" is his comment and at least he doesn't flat out refuse to wear it. In town a lady stops to speak to Will and he is very unfriendly. We had previously had a talk about Valentine's Day being about love and that he should be nice to people. When we drive away I remind him of our talk and he says, "Me nice to D and Daddy!" I guess I wanted him to spread the love too far.

Once back home we do spend lots of time outside. He continues digging a deep hole in the sand box. We then play golf in the front yard and both enjoy it. He has a darling habit of throwing kisses to his many admirers when he scores. I somehow doubt that he got that from Tiger Woods. He finally tires and we go inside to play the fish game.

Will wants Wes to leave because we are not finished playing. I take it as the supreme compliment that it is. We play more and he lines up every weapon in the house to fight multiple "mean" guys. He even brings in the dogs because they can bite the mean guys. He has a hat in case it gets cold. He is nothing if not prepared. Wes comes back at six and has to get a quick bath and go to town for T-ball registration. It is that time again. I ended up enjoying it last year and maybe things will be even more comfortable this time around.

A Long Line of Pranksters...

I come from a long line of pranksters. I can only assume it's in our DNA, especially exhibited in our males.

When Will was a toddler, our family finances were especially tight. My eyes are sun sensitive and at the worst possible time, I broke my sunglasses. I scraped up the money to order some new sunglasses from Jane Lamb. That purchase really strained the budget. I was very proud of my new glasses. The first week I had the glasses, I lost them. I turned the car inside out. I moved every couch cushion at my house and at Wes's. I called every business and place I had visited in town that day. I even called the Police Station, in case they had fallen into the street. No luck! Finally I did what often works, I cried. So I ended up with puffy eyes I needed to hide behind sunglasses. Will watched my hissy fit that went on for hours. Finally as I was tossing Will's toys into his toy box, I caught a glimpse of the glasses' case buried beneath trucks and stuffed animals. I grabbed my glasses, clutched them to my chest, and screamed, "Will Davis!" He grinned up at me with a very familiar smirk and said, "Me got Ya Ya!" Yes, he did.

Chill Down

"Chill down, Ya-Ya" One of Will's favorite little smart aleck things when he was about three and a half.

Will is on a talking jag and fires everyone in the family. It is so funny. I don't think that he came from Donald Trump. The boss on Cat In The Hat fires lots of people and most likely that is where it came from. He fired Wes and me and I explain that I don't work. He even fires Mama Mary and then he says that all old Mamas are fired. Old Mamas means old women. That might suit most of us. Wes laughs and says when he gets started like this that it just goes on and on.

Will Stories

Monday and I didn't expect to have Will, but it is a treat. He is wide awake when I get down to Wes's and Wes says that he has already asked, "Where Ya-Ya?". I love it. He loves having a full-service grandmother and I bring him juice and food and try to make him happy. He wants me to play the fish game on the computer and then turn it over to him when it gets to the point that the fish can eat anything that swims. He is presently enthralled with eights and looks for them everytime that the game ends. We have no problem filling up the morning. I have him washed and cleaned and teeth brushed when Ashley picks him up.

I call the ALF and Joy, the nice volunteer, brings Mama to the door. It is a thrill for Mama to touch Will and really get a close up look at him. She tells me many times just how cute he is. This is the only time that he is still and he is sleeping so hard that he is drooling down his shirt.

Will telling just how dark the new enclosed tube sliding board is. As he said, no little dark, but big dark.

Vanilla milkshake from the Chicken Shack is described as "not choc choc".

We play outside blowing bubbles for a few minutes. Then Will gets on the Gator and I realize that Wes has changed the speed so that it flies. Will drives around the house and I have to hurry to keep up with him. I know that I need the exercise and the day is pleasant. He makes at least five trips and then the power starts to fade on the Gator. My power also started to fade at about the same time. I talk Will into going inside and we start a Scooby Doo DVD. I settle in the rocking chair and he sits and plays around.

Life is Will

Will comes to stay with me. I tell him that we can paint and we drag out the paints and he spends over an hour doing pictures. Today his theme is coyotes and friendly snakes. Whatever. We also go over to my bedroom and play some handheld poker and watch cartoons.

Four year old Will asks if I am mean which translates am I mad. I guess not, but it takes forever to set up a video game from scratch. He has a new thing of saying, "Trust me." Yea, right.

I go in and take a long look at the baby boy.. He is flat on his back and has his arms spread out to his sides. He is beautiful and I love him beyond belief. There won't be another one like him. He makes me work so hard for his affection. He has been like that toward me since birth. He was born playing hard to get. I think of all the masculine men in our family tree....Duzzer, W.R..... and know that they would be proud of him. He is all man.

We go into the bedroom and Will terrifies me going up and down the new bunk bed ladder. I am really going to enjoy this new deal and he asks me if I hate it. He knows that I will worry about him falling and he will love the fact that I worry. Boys!

Will has to play hiding under the comforter on the big bed. That is the only time that he will cuddle. We also have two imaginary E.T.s and two dogs with us. He puts his little head that smells so good right on my shoulder and we hide from "mean guys". I try to explain the difference in real mean guys and play like mean guys and maybe he gets it. Anyway he says, "Me and Ya-Ya safe now." I almost tear up because maybe we are safe for a little while. I wouldn't take any amount of money for this time that we have had together.

After movie watching, we go outside and feed the horses grass and weeds. Will wants to feed gravel to the horses and when I tell him that they don't eat rocks, he asks me how I knew that. It was so cute. Later in the sandbox he told me that he knew everything, "all", and asks me if I know all. I told him that I knew a lot, but that I didn't know all.

One thing that went on today that was precious was when Will wanted me to play hiding with him. We snuggled down under the striped bedspread and were hiding from monsters. There were times that Will would leave his old grandmamma hidden and he would go fight monsters and then come back to me. He would even put his little buzz cut head on my shoulder and for some reason give in to the body contact. He demonstrated that he could squat and run to the end of the bed and back. He encouraged me to try that but I declined. He does consider me a playmate. There was something so intimate and sweet about being with him under the big, thick spread that just touched me. I try hard to soak up our time together because I saw how fast the last school year went by and this time next year he will probably be going to K-4 and he won't be my playmate anymore.

Will still uses lots of sign language and his own special way of short speak. He keeps turning on the clock radio and putting the volume switch just as loud as possible. When I can stand it no more I unplug the radio and find that it has battery backup and it keeps playing. When he sees that I am looking to see just how hard it would be to remove the battery, he goes nuts. He comes out with a sermon that lets me know that when it gets "dark outsize", one of his favorite phrases, that his Daddy goes to sleep and needs that radio to get up in the morning. He shows me how Wes bangs on the snooze button and that he is going to be so mad at Ya-Ya that he is going to spank her. He demonstrates everything for me, especially the mad face and the spanking that I am going to receive for my transgression. I get the message.

He can communicate extremely well considering that he rarely speaks true language. I know that he needs to be with other children, but I don't think that Wes or Ashley are ready to rush that. Sometimes I just have to sit on my ideas.

On my way to nursing class:

This morning getting behind the school buses was such a thrill. I enjoyed watching the kids bounce on the bus when it stopped. Watching the mothers' faces was both enlightening and nostalgic for me. Every mother had that hopeful, but doubtful look that goes along with sending your chicks out into the big, bad world. The bus stops on the highway at a dusty country road. No child is in sight, but in a moment a little red car roars down the trail stirring up the dust and then slams on brakes. A pudgy elementary age boy hops out and scurries up the bus steps. He never looks back and his mother watches wistfully as the bus pulls away. Somehow I suspect that this is not the last time this particular red car will speed up to the bus stop. There is a country store at the lake with several mothers in cars waiting with children for the bus. No child appears to be wearing crisp, new clothes because that is not the style. All the denim looks like it has been passed through the family ranks for decades.

I know that my time is coming with Will. One more year and he will be in K4 and I will be....... Where? Don't even know. Will Julie have a baby by then and need me or will I have lots of free time and leisure? Will I drop him off at school or pick him up or both? Will Mama still be at Assisted Living or will she finally get to die and go, as she puts it? So many questions and very few answers.

When I get to the class one of the young nurses asks if she can leave her cell phone on because she has a sick child. Been there and done that. I remember starting school one year and being at the summer conference in Montgomery when we were in a tiny room at the Eight Days Inn with Wes burning up with fever and hallucinating. Mama was with me to look after the kids while I met my job requirements of attending boring, tedious workshops. I remember lying in the dark with my flaming baby and wondering if I would live through another school year. Now Wes is 30 and I made it to retirement and now…..I am keeping Wes's baby on a daily basis and checking his temperature and wondering if I will survive it. Once a mother, always a mother.

He Loves to Read

Yesterday afternoon Will and I sat in the car under the big tree in the parking lot at the Methodist Church. We were a little early for the Wednesday night events to begin.

I had the windows open and there was a gentle breeze blowing. We both had our phones out. I sent a short text and then pulled out the new John Grisham novel and started to read. In a few minutes, Will put down his cell phone and picked up a thick book he had just checked out at the public library.

It hit me that, for a grandmother, it just doesn't get any better than that moment. When Will was little, he never wanted to sit still and let me read to him. When he got older, I worried that he was too involved in video games. Early on, he didn't seem to thrive in the reading program at the school. All that didn't matter one bit at this perfect moment. He loves to read. I love to read. I reached over and patted his arm. Neither one of us said a word. We didn't need to.

The Chicken Noodle Stuff

I picked up Will after his first day of school. He got off to a really good start. He ran my errands in town and on the way home, he said, " Ya Ya, remember that chicken noodle stuff you make that we all love?" I replied, "I sure do. That casserole is really good on a chilly night, later in the fall." And my clever grandson says, "Ya Ya, that stuff is delicious, no matter what the weather is like!" Being a grandmother is the absolute best! It's being manipulated and loving it! You know what's coming.

Fine

I stayed excited all day Monday as I relived another first day Back To School. I so enjoyed all the pictures and the cute comments on Facebook as I waited for the school day to end. Around four I got the call I had so anticipated. When I asked Will, "How was your first day of high school?" Will's response was "Fine." Grandmothers so need details and grandsons don't. At least he had no complaints! Have a great year everyone.

The Headsets

Glad I can laugh at myself. I kept Will this weekend. I bragged to Billy that our grandson had such a wonderful imagination. I kept hearing him talk to what I assumed were imaginary friends. The next day I went in his room and he had on a headset and was talking to "real" kids who were playing a video game with him thru the Internet. Nothing like a grandmother to be old and out of it!

****

He sits in the high chair when we get home and eats lots of my grilled chicken and then he finishes up with ice cream. We have to get out all the matchbox trucks and the little computer board that has numbers and letters. He spends longer on that than I ever would have thought. We then go play in my bed and he comes up with a new game that involves him running out of power and me fixing him with lotion and powder. He must have said, "Me broke." a dozen times.

We play hiding place, Will's new favorite game after he gets up about ten. He eats most of a yeast roll and drinks lots of Ya-Ya juice. Kay comes later to look at the pictures and she agrees that Will is rowdy in the proofs. She and I both think that he needs to be around other children and needs some consistent discipline. Not that it matters what we think. Billy is fretting that I might confine him in some way, but he eventually comes to get us after eating breakfast and lunch, only a salad, with the guys. We eat grilled chicken salad at the Mexican and Will behaves really well for Billy. He eats a lot and we head on to Brantley to the bank. The day is muggy, dark, and overcast. It starts to rain right when we get to Brantley. Billy has to go in to rework a trucking loan and we sit in the truck through a raging thunderstorm. Billy could not possibly come out due to the lightning. Will dances, plays air guitar, regulates the windshield wipers and finds the flashlights. He is cute, energetic, and not too rough. Finally Billy comes out and takes us home.

We do the post office, cleaners, bank, and drugstore and get even more ready to head to the beach tomorrow morning. Will cries to drive and tells Billy a long list of family members who let him drive on the highway. What a joke! Billy lets him drive on the farm and he loves speed and rowdiness. No surprises. We go back to Jim's to watch the crew take down tree limbs. They have already removed the dead tree in Jim's front yard. Will is disappointed that they aren't running the chain saws. Wes calls and needs Billy to come move the boat from the shop. We do and Will is very glad to see his Daddy. Will and I ride in the boat while Billy pulls it. Will pretends to be scared and needs to hold my hand. I give Will his last kiss before we leave for our trip. Billy gets sugar, too. I dread the time away, but I have to have some life on my own. I absolutely adore him and I want to be there for him all the time.

Will starts dragging out all sorts of stuff. There isn't much method to his madness. He just feels better when surrounded by clutter. He does watch most of Lion King, but wakes me up when I snooze and demands that I not sleep. I miss my paperback novel and hunt and hunt. I ask Will about it and he knows nothing. I think to look in his briefcase and he has hidden it from me. The little rascal! We waste most of the afternoon and Billy comes back around four. We load up to play and Billy sees Wes pulling in from 331 about the time we turn in from the Airport Road. Will and Wes are so glad to see each other that it is touching. They both just light up. Will drives Wes's Jeep home and he and Billy play chicken. I can see why he is such a wild child because his father and grandfather encourage it. I am old.

Life is...
Pretzel

Pretzel

She was a miniature salt and pepper schnauzer, who lived a little more than ten years and she was so, so much more. I want to write down everything I can remember and I want to be able to tell my grandchildren about Pretzel.

I came up with the name because the word "pretzel" is German and so are schnauzers. The name originated from the Latin word "Pretiola" which means little reward. A monk, as a gift to children for learning their prayers, created pretzels.

We bought her from a couple in Montgomery who had a matched set of schnauzers. I don't remember what Wes paid for her, but I am sure that he remembers to the penny. In my mind, she has always been mine. She recognized everybody's name except I don't think she had a name for me. I think I was just basically there and I was the one who said, "I hear Daddy." And "Where's Wes?" It was just one of the many games that we played.

Ballet stretch

Tapping our heels with the tips of her nails

to show how much she loved us

Tapping the doors with her nails to get in

Refusing to go outside unless it was her idea

Wallowing on her back when she was overcome with joy

(The Willie Wagga)

Chewing and eating anything with our body fluids present

Liking to play with an empty paper towel holder

Doing a back flip when she was younger....like a little circus dog

Sliding on the wax on the kitchen floor

Life is Pretzel

Chewing the corners off the back steps when she was a teething puppy

Chewing those nylon bones and holding them daintily in her front paws

Taking out the trash can with Billy on Sunday nights

Going out to "see Kay" at the office everyday when I got home from work

Having that funny look when you picked her up to cuddle her. She was not a cuddler.

Resting her chin on her crossed paws

Hating to see a suitcase

Loving to play hide and seek with me

Getting stuck under the house

Getting stuck under the screen cover for the drain

Coming back on the back porch and nuzzling around in her tin pan and making that familiar noise so that I always knew she was back from her after meal run

The nightly ritual of bringing Daddy in the house when he got out of his truck.

The way that she understood to stay on the porch until he cut the engine

That look she had when she wanted people to leave so we could go to bed

That hopeful look she had every time you opened a bread product

Her demanding bark for a piece of ice when Billy fixed his cocktail. He had to pretend to drop it. It wasn't nearly as much fun if he just gave her a piece.

The way she thought that the birds and squirrels were underlings

The way she resented a chipmunk

The way she growled at black birds.

Her three special spots: The corner of the couch, behind the sheers at the living room sliding glass door and the fuzzy blanket that she took away from Billy for her spot in front of our bedroom window. And don't forget that special spot in our hearts that will always be a little bit empty

Overlooking her kingdom like royalty

That special sigh that she had.... boredom or contentment.... we never knew

That dog cursing that she gave me every time I picked her up from the vet.

The way she shook and yawned from stress every time we took her to the vet and when she heard the left blinker noise, the way that she acted.

How thrilled she was when I turned into the driveway to bring her back home.

Treating those ear mites

Scratching her butt on the edge of the glass coffee table

The way we had to put the trash cans on the back of the commodes to keep her out of them

The way that she would unmake the beds and scatter the pillows to the floor. One time Bob thought that we had had a burglar come in and sleep in the guest room because the bed was unmade

The way she scratched like she was digging a hole on the couch and in the middle of my bed and she scratched that huge hole in the cushion on the couch in the playroom

The way that she would lay on that cold tile floor in the playroom

The way she would follow me from room to room....no matter what I was doing

The way she would finally give up and go to bed if we stayed up too late

That special sound she made when she was running hard to come back after I called her into the house

The way my heart would feel when she took too long coming back to the house that was just a warning of how I would feel when she left for good......Pretzel pain. Also I could feel my blood pressure soar when she wouldn't come and she wouldn't come and that was usually on a night when it was 20 degrees and I wasn't dressed to go hunting her. Actually it would be such a relief when she showed up that I couldn't truly stay mad at her.

Life is Pretzel

The crazy way she treated all my family.....she didn't like Mama Mary much and Mama insisted on calling her "him". We all got a kick out of that.

The way she loved on Bob, stretching up his leg and making weird noises when he came up for coffee on the last weekend of her life.

The way that she always seemed to remember the way Tom played with her when she was a puppy and like most females, she seemed to always carry a crush for him

The way she knew Julie was part of the immediate family even when she didn't see her for months.

The way she smelled when she needed a bath and the way she smelled and felt when she came home from grooming.

She peed several times on the floor next to my chair in the computer room because I think she had had enough of me sitting in that spot and ignoring her

The way she was waiting for me at the back door every day when I came in from school

The way she would jump up and look out at us when we came home. So happy to see us and so excited.

The way that she worshipped a routine, regular day.....when we did everything as usual and had nothing out of the ordinary. A stay at home day.

The way that she loved summers....when teachers stayed home all day.

The elation she exhibited when I would come home from a long trip to Atlanta and she just went crazy like she had almost lost hope that I was coming back.

The way she thought the Christmas tree was an imposition because we moved the furniture around and took over her spot in front of the living room glass door

The precious way she cocked her head to side, just like the old RCA dog, in an attempt to understand something you were asking her

The way she would pretend to be mad and refuse eye contact when we were "play" fighting......her special fierce look....all for fun

The way she would pretend to bite you and cover your hand with her teeth and not put one bit of pressure behind it.

The way she was afraid of Ashley because Ashley was so unpredictable.

The way she could pee in 5 seconds if it was pouring down rain and the way she could take forever if I was in a hurry.

The funny way she looked when she walked out in a snowy backyard, sort of like I didn't sign up for this as a southern puppy.

The way she was afraid of Billy if he got harsh.

The way I could say "I'm gonna tell Daddy." And she acted just like a child at that warning.

The way she turned a trip from the kitchen to the bedroom into a race that she always won. She would pass me as soon as I got to the bedroom hall door.

The way she tried to jump-start me in the mornings.....making a run for the kitchen and then stopping and coming back and trying it again ...until the dummy got the idea.

The way that she thought I had lost my mind on Monday mornings because I was waiting until the trash truck left and she thought I had forgotten to feed her. Then if I let her go out to eat and then wouldn't let her go down the truck drive to do her business....then she would show me and you couldn't get her to go out once the trash run was finished. There was no way I could win on Monday mornings.

Pretzel getting into the dish washer and licking the plates

The way she was our full time door bell, barking and barking endlessly at anyone who came to the door.

Life is...
Holidays.

Saw a stocking stuffer feature on the Today Show for $20+ items. In my family that is a "good" gift.

I was raised in a family where stockings were filled with what Mama Mary charmingly referred to as junk. She was not kidding. Space fillers like tangerines and those candy canes the size of fire logs worked well.

Mama once told me that Daddy Guy was upset when they could only afford used bicycles. I was perfectly satisfied with my ride. First thing I did was paint it.... hapharzardly, with paint I found in the basement. Bob used to ride his down the front steps of the Methodist Church. Daddy worried needlessly. New bikes are wasted on some kids.

My point is....I've never been disappointed on Christmas. Merry Christmas! Do it your way!

LUMC Christmas Cantata

So enjoyed the Luverne United Methodist Church Christmas Cantata. Loved visiting with some old family friends and listening to some of the most beautiful voices in our community. Thought of my Mother and what this church meant to her. Perdues used to fill the altar railing for Communion on Christmas Eve. Those days are gone, but the memories are precious. Merry Christmas!

****

The Naked Christmas Tree

How can I not love you, my Facebook friends? I post a naked Christmas tree straight out of the box and you kind, understanding people compliment it, like it, and are totally tolerant. Somehow I figure when Billy goes to town for coffee this morning several folks are going to ask...How's Miss Pat doing? I have a weird sense of humor. Born with it. Hope I die with it.

I was selected Wittiest Girl in Junior High at Luverne School back in the early 60s. I was good with it, but Daddy said that is another way of saying you are driving those teachers crazy. Stop it! Sorry, Daddy, I won't change, ever.

Hope you guys know that I know my naked tree is unacceptable. The day is looming when I won't know the difference. If you see me in Super Foods wearing my fuzzy slippers, call Billy. If you see me in the middle of 331, buck naked, just like my tree, call the police. They know what to do with me. Do tell them to bring a large blanket and an open mind. Life is Good!

****

Nothing is probably my perfect day. Candles, Christmas tree lights, Christmas music on cable, mulling spice, chicken soup, hot coffee, warm socks. Merry Christmas everybody! Do it your way!

****

Yesterday was as close to perfect as a rainy day gets. Had all three of my guys here for lots of the day. Had willing helpers to get the tree down. Had lots of wonderful leftovers. Made delicious soup. Finally got word our daughter, SIL, and grandpuppy made it safely home from San Antonio area to Atlanta.

Billy and I ended the night watching a brand new Western and, hang onto your hats, followed by a Nicholas Sparks movie. Call it date night, senior citizen style. We stayed awake through two movies. We share everything, but I would have been perfectly fine without Billy's cold.

For better or worse, in sickness and health, and all that jazz. Life is Crazy Good!

****

Our son, nearly 40 years ago in his bean bag chair with his ba ba and his beloved "Monkney". Made him this ornament so that every Christmas he will be reminded that he is forever our baby boy. Merry Christmas.

****

Christmas Day marked 60 years of WSFA 12 News being on the air...

I was 7 years old. I stretched out on the floor in the den at my grandparents home on Hiway 331, north of Luverne and waited impatiently for Channel 12 to come on the screen of their small black and white television. WSFA has been a huge part of day-to-day life!

****

The Morning After

I sort of like the morning after. Tree lit one last time. Burning the last of the Christmas candle. Drinking my coffee from a Christmas mug before I pack them away. Looking through our Christmas cards one more time. Good time to reflect and appreciate my life! Hope you and yours had a great Christmas and are headed toward a Happy 2016! Life is Crazy Good!

Life is... Holidays.

Will's last Santa picture. Been 4-5 years ago. I had to beg and bribe to get this one. I love it, frame it and cherish it during this season. With a single grandchild, there are no do overs.

My greatest gift is the privilege of being a grandmother, who lived close by and had daily contact all through his elementary years.

Nothing better in life. Life is Crazy Good! Merry Christmas to my Facebook friends and family!

****

Donny's Rabbits

Sunday morning treasures. Easter is three weeks away. Donny Ray Holmes brought up some plants he saved for me in his green house. Friday he gave me two solid glass, antique Easter Bunnies that have been in his family for years and years. He is not a man who heeds the word "No". I am humbled by such special gifts. Today he finds a tiny bird egg on a lawn chair in my garage. Made a pretty tableau. I don't why the egg is unbroken. I don't know why he gives me his family heirlooms. Life is a mystery on the Airport Road.

Donny's Rabbits, part 2

Mystery solved! Cowbirds fly in and eat my scattered birdseed. Donny Ray Holmes researched and found that cowbirds are home wreckers. They move the eggs out of the nests of other birds and use the nests for their own purposes. Who knew? Thought this was limited to human behavior. Who suffers? The three little birds who missed the warmth and nurturing in the family nest. Pretty deep for one cup of coffee on a Monday morning.

Life is... Holidays.

Boring Valentine

When I was 17 if I could have looked at my Valentine's weekend fifty years in the future.....well, I would have thought I was the most boring person in the world! Thank God for boring! The most wonderful gifts are love, peace, quiet, and trust.

****

How can I be 70 and still remember my Easter basket? Nothing fancy and a little bit crooked, but I remember it had lots of purple to it. We used the same baskets until we outgrew the Easter bunny. Actually I think they lasted until we each grew up and left home. Mama made sure my basket was a little bit bigger than Bob's whose was a little bit bigger than Jim's whose was a little bit bigger than Tom's.

We loved the process of dying eggs. The steaming hot water and the combination of vinegar and those magic little pills that filled six coffee cups. There were several packs of Easter egg dye because there would be spills. I recall that wire utensil that allowed retrieval of eggs from the hot mixture. We would fight over whose turn it was to use a particular color, the wire utensil, the best, unbroken eggs. We were loud, rowdy, and we fought a lot. We also laughed a lot.

Every year I made an egg that was half pink and half blue. I had to get the colors just right. The longer you left the egg immersed, the deeper the colors. Every year when we finished dying eggs, my brothers mixed the cooling cups of dye and attempted to make the ugliest color ever. That was a boy thing.

Each child claimed six completed, perfect Easter eggs. We always ate the left over cracked eggs. The tradition was that we filled two egg cartons with our completed dyed eggs on the kitchen counter the night before Easter. We had no problem believing that the Easter bunny put these very same eggs in our baskets on Easter morning. There was no individually wrapped Easter candy when we were kids. There were jellybean eggs, chocolate eggs, Pez dispensers, and Peeps. We dug our treats out of that cellophane grass and everything was delicious. We each got a hollow

146

chocolate bunny. Mine always had a pink hair bow. The boys' had a blue bow tie. There were no treats that didn't snuggly fit in our baskets.

There were no toys, books, or unexpected surprises. We actually got to eat junk for Easter breakfast. We couldn't linger over Easter treats. Four kids were somehow properly dressed in our Easter finery. We were one of the first families to arrive at the Methodist Church. We sang the traditional Easter songs and squirmed through an Easter sermon. We knew the Easter story, but arising from death didn't seem that dramatic because we didn't know death. We didn't know divorce or sorrow or loss. The Perdues knew tradition and Life was Good! Happy Easter to my Facebook family.

****

Just another little Perdue Easter story. About the time I was getting ready to graduate from Luverne High School, our grandmother, Annie Lou Folmar Perdue, had our usual grandchild egg hunt planned for Easter Sunday afternoon.

This year rather than hold this hunt in her back yard, Mamaw decided to hide the eggs along dam of the new Perdue fish pond on Odum's Bridge Road. This road is now Airport Road. All of us, my three brothers and our two female first cousins, showed up at the appointed time. We were all teens or mighty close to it.

Will never forget the sight of my big brother, Bob Perdue, a pretty powerful defensive tackle for the Luverne Tigers, as he toted that basket and searched for Mamaw's carefully hidden Easter eggs. He did whisper to me, "I hope nobody on the team rides by."

The things we do for love. None of us would have dreamed of hurting Mamaw's feelings by refusing to participate. Proud to have grown up that way.

****

Thanksgiving 2000

The Wednesday before Thanksgiving was a no school day. I had had the luxury of a very competent house cleaning service on the day before school let out. I was enjoying my second cup of coffee and patting myself on the back and thinking that I had things pretty much under control. Big Mistake! First time I turned on the stove it started smoking and set off the smoke alarm, which happens to be located too high to reach without a ladder. This must have gone on for at least five minutes until the mist cleared. As I stopped to take an Advil, I noticed that the water was not draining from the kitchen sink. After plunging and pouring boiling water down the drain, in desperation I spooned the directed amount of Drano down the sink and went over to make the beds and tidy up the living room. Back in the kitchen there developed a small leak under the sink where the Drano had eaten numerous holes in a very old pipe. When I re-entered, greasy water was running across the room and covering the freshly waxed floor. Under the sink was a five-year accumulation of cheap florist vases and ribbons, bottles half filled with flat soda, and half-dozen cans of very stale beer. You know the type family treasures to which we find ourselves so thoroughly emotionally attached. I promptly donned heavy-duty work gloves, stood on my head for thirty minutes, and cleaned up that disaster. Then I called my good son to come rescue me. Within a couple of minutes Wes and several mechanic's helpers were dragging leaking pipes and rusted fittings through my previously clean house. In due time we accumulated more manpower, tools, and dirty work boots. When Bob showed up with a crowbar and the male contingent started ripping away at the wallboards in the den, by popular demand, I made a grocery store run.

The moral of this tale is you might be a redneck if you are catching your dishwater in five gallon buckets and slinging soap suds out the back door while you serve 40+ a holiday meal. In spite of it all, we had a great time and basked in the glory of family togetherness. Did I mention that the temperature was in the 20's and we had mounted a truck tarp to surround the patio area? Holiday décor you will not encounter watching Martha Stewart. The crowd consumed gallons of gumbo, mounds of fried fish, and oysters on the half shell. The next morning my immediate family went to Destin and spent the rest of the Thanksgiving break with smoothly functioning plumbing and a refreshing lack of stress.

****

The first metallic tree I ever saw was at a slumber party at Suzette's house. A large group of giggling girls bedded down on the floor in the living room midst sleeping bags and quilts. The revolving wheel changed the tree colors all night long. It was surreal and absolutely beautiful. I remember that we celebrated Suzette's birthday along with Christmas. We brought Suzette individual gifts and had drawn names and had a price limit on Christmas gifts. I believe anything over a couple of dollars was a big no-no. Life was so simple then. School was out for Christmas break. We were happy, excited, and as carefree as we would probably ever be again. Funny what sticks in your head when you get old. Merry Christmas!

****

One more holiday post I wanted to share while I still had a little remaining Christmas spirit. 20 things I remember about our special Christmases in the 1950-60s in Luverne, Alabama.

1. The city had strings of colored lights stretched across main street.

2. Most Christmas trees were real and were not put up too early because they would dry out and shed.

3. Christmas had its own magical aroma that no longer exists.

4. If one Christmas light went out on your tree, they all went out.

5. We used icicles on our tree that stuck to our clothes due to static electricity and were scattered throughout the house.

6. We had short, reasonable Christmas lists. We actually worried about Santa skipping the stop at our house.

7. I remember the first Christmas card we received with pictures of the senders and their names in print. They were rich and the cards

were very expensive.

8. Christmas clothes were red or green sweat shirts. Period.

9. When we gathered food for a local, poor family, we personally knew them and the circumstances that made them needy.

10. If you received a gift that you did not want, you faked gratitude and were careful not to hurt anyone's feelings.

11. The Sears catalog was the gold standard for wish lists.

12. We discreetly drew names in our circle of school friends and gifts never cost more than a couple of dollars.

13. Mama and Daddy always went to the annual Lions Club Christmas party and dressed to the nines. The wives were given poinsettias after the party and Mama proudly displayed hers on our mantle.

14. Every single time a children's Christmas choir was formed, the kids wore white, simple homemade robes with red bows at the neck. These were passed down in the family for years. A brand new robe stood out like a sore thumb. Too white!

15. There were no gift bags. Everything was wrapped. The Fair Store and English's had wrapping stations.

16. Every family had a nativity scene as part of their decorations.

17. Most people shopped in Luverne and only went to Montgomery for special items.

18. Families piled into their cars to ride around and look at Christmas lights at least once during Christmas week.

19. All the kids I knew really and truly believed in Santa Claus.

20. Christmas Eve communion was extra special. I loved watching church families exchange greetings and hugs on the front steps of our candle lit church. In those days, I knew every family.

Hope this stirs a few special memories before they get packed away. Happy New Year!

Life is...
Gratitude.

Thankful

November. I am thankful to live in the Deep South. I love the accents, the personalities, and the food. I would not want to live anywhere else. Bloom where you are planted. Deep roots and deep affection!

****

I am more thankful than ever for the ability to laugh, especially good to laugh at ourselves. Look at it as self defense. Ha, ha, ha!

****

I am forever thankful for ending up with my classmate, my old friend, my life's partner. Now that we are easing up on 50 years together, we often encounter younger folks who want to know our secret. No secret. Neither one of us ever left. We got mad, ticked off, fed up. We never got violent. If you get angry enough to feel the top of your skull about to launch towards the sky, that's your sign. That's real love! Intense emotions equal love.

I also notice on a day that I think I might be coming down with the flu, a cold, a virus and then 30 minutes after Billy walks in the back door....I am miraculously healed. That is love.

One more thing, when I hear his pickup pull into the carport and feel my heart do that little skipped beat thing that it did when I was 20 years old, well, that is love. I am truly thankful for Billy Davis.

****

Life is... Gratitude.

Thankful for our mother. We lost her November 24, 2007.. She was everything she needed to be for the four of us. She was tough, fair, and as scary as a coiled rattlesnake. Ask any of her four children and they would tell you basically the same thing....Don't mess with Mama!

Many, many people knew her as a sweet, caring, Godly woman. She was, but she set the bar mighty high for her kids. Thankful for Mama Mary.

****

Huge day, but I made it. Bought 11 quarts of stew. That should get me to the end of football season. Only 30 people at the Memorial Service today. I could feel Mamaw's approval that Jim, Tom, and I represented our family. Very nice spread afterwards. I think from Chappy's deli.

Homemade pimento cheese and egg salad and a beautiful fruit tray. We didn't even go to a restaurant. Jim had a Cabinet Meeting with the Governor. Tom and I just came on home.

****

Day 9: Thankful for peace and contentment. The older I get, the greater the gift.

****

Thankful to live in the South. Nice to wake up on a rainy Sunday morning and read joyous facebook posts from pleased football fans. Do we even realize how lucky we are? In other parts of the world, families woke up to search for food, clean water, adequate clothing, and decent shelter. Please let us be aware of our blessed lives in a great country. May we never take it for granted. Enjoy the fact that our biggest problem this weekend may have been a football score and having a fresh shirt with our favorite team logo. The very least we can all do is be grateful.

****

I am thankful to be a grandmother. This role gives a woman the rare chance for a do-over that is both fun and pretty much fail proof!

****

Thankful to be an early riser! Thankful for hot coffee, sunrises, and quiet time! Being comfortable in your own skin is a tremendous gift! There are many blessings in a regular, ordinary day!

****

Who is even better than Santa Claus? Donny Ray Holmes is the best friend and the best neighbor. He makes my life beautiful. Thank you so much!

****

I made it just fine without a sister. I learned valuable life skills in the management of the Southern male. I learned how to fight without crying. Wouldn't change a thing.

****

I am thankful for plans, to-do lists, and something to look forward to everyday. Life is Good! And one more thing, thankful for all the extended family that I have found on Facebook. You make life sweeter!

****

Thankful that my life has been filled with more laughter than tears.

****

I was 16 years old and in the junior class at Luverne High School. We had finished lunch and I was headed to the gym. Someone shouted, "The President has been shot!" I grew up a lot on November 22nd and realized that the world can be a scary place. Today, at 68, I feel that fear again. God Bless the U.S.A.!

****

I am thankful that I am very seldom mad about anything. Life is too sweet to waste time being angry. Think age took care of that bad habit.

****

Thanksgiving season is done. I won't be posting any more daily gratitude comments, BUT I will still be feeling it. Really got a boost out of giving my personal abundance deliberate thought and sharing those with you. Enjoy the rest of the holiday season with your family and friends. Life is so Good!

****

I gave Mama Mary her due last week. Made sure to get that big American flag to the cemetery prior to Veterans Day. Yes, Mama, I made sure there was no flag larger than yours on a male Veterans grave. Size mattered to her. I even made it to the outstanding Veterans Day Program at the school. I stood up tall at all appropriate moments and put my hand over my heart during The Pledge.

Yesterday I took my Hardee's biscuit and coffee out to the cemetery. I parked my car by Mama and had my breakfast. There was a nice breeze and birds chirping in the nearby trees. She's been gone nine years next week. It's taken me about that long to get past those four years of hell. Dementia is properly named. A devil that steals everything. Never would have thought I could give up my mother and not shed a tear. I did have my tears, but they were long gone. Dried up, when that empty shell left this earth.

But finally, finally I have gotten back some of the good family memories. So I pulled up her flag and swept some scattered leaves and dust from her bronze military plaque.

Happy Thanksgiving, Mama! It's all good down here. You finally have a few more great grands and another on the way. I don't blame you for the arthritis because I got plenty of your good stuff, too. Doing the best I can. I hear you whisper in my ear pretty regularly. Rest in Peace.

****

Today I am so thankful to have options and the right to make choices. When I mess up....it is on me and I am woman enough to live with it! Billy is not on facebook so he will not read this! Almost like admitting I can make mistakes!

Life is... Gratitude.

Thankful for passion in all its forms. May my fire last as long as I do. Amen.

****

So thankful for our Veterans - young and old, male and female, here with us and gone! Forgive us for the days we take our freedoms for granted!

****

Don't know that I ever really slept last night. I was piddling on Google and looked for a catchy phrase about unity. The following verse repeatedly popped up, to the point, I actually wondered if Mama Mary had taken control of the Internet. Don't laugh. She blinked the lights during her funeral to remind us she was still our Matriarch.

I have never posted a Bible verse on Facebook. I diligently avoid public religious and political arguments, but this morning I feel that Mama insisted.

"Come now, and let us reason together, says the Lord." We hear you, Mama.

****

Thankful for leftovers including time leftover to spend with family. The best feeling for a mother is to have her family under one roof and to go to sleep to the sound of the laughter of her adult children. It gets no better.

****

Weather radar looks spooky. Get it done and cuddle up safely at home. Don't have a jack o lantern, but orange candles work for me.

I lit them last night. Billy asked, "Why are the candles lit?" I didn't have a good answer for that one. I just smiled and mumbled. Works really well with old men. Life is Good! Happy Halloween!

* * * * * * * * * * * * * * *

I am thankful that I am content with who I am, where I am, and who is with me. Pretty much sums up my life.

* *

Thankful for family. Thankful for a long list of folks to worry over. Real thankful to be the older generation. No denying it when you have buried both parents. Being old is a privilege. Most of it is fun, but some of it is a nuisance.

I appreciate where I am. Short bucket list. Long gratitude list.

* * * * * * * * * * * *

I am thankful for having flowers and plants year round. I planted mostly pretty pansies and veggies last week. Flowers are a gift I give myself. My fingernails are dirty and ragged this morning. My back and knees are stiff, but it was so worth it! Small pleasures.

* * * * * * * * * * * * * * * * * * * *

The worst advice ever written in a high school yearbook. "Stay the same." God help the few who haven't changed. Long live the Class of '65!

* *

I am filled with gratitude for all the important things that involve family, health, and abundance. I am also thankful for the little things like the fact that Dillard's has an attractive line of slacks with elastic waist bands and built-in lycra.

****

Consider letting your gray hair win. You can get away with so much with a head full of gray hair. Better than bail money.

****

I am thankful for family. Family is messy, loud, and at times, a bunch of trouble. Who wants a neat life? Love = Family! Thankful that I have not had a predictable, orderly life.

****

Thankful to have a good man who has made a wonderful husband, a sensitive, loving father, and a goofy granddaddy. Decisions made at age 20 don't all turn out this well! Thankful for love and luck!

****

I am thankful for all the men in my family who know how to do stuff. I take it for granted that they can fix things, solve problems, drive anything that runs, and keep me a little bit spoiled. Feels good!

****

Thankful that Life is Good! I am thankful for friends, Facebook and face to face, who appear to love me in spite of myself. I have so many faults. I am a such a braggart. Guess they accept that most of my comments come from boundless love for spouse and family.

I am also a Pollyanna to the extreme. Life is Good and thanks to you folks who get me.

****

I am thankful to be here. I am actually okay with the gray hair and the wrinkles and the slower pace. We have lost friends too young, too soon. We both realize that this extra time is a true gift!

****

This woman In the beauty shop said she is 81 and has 3 gardens. Thank goodness I kept my mouth shut.

If you have to do it, why do you brag about it? If you count the packs you put in the freezer, why? Once I want to hear a woman say that she had sex a dozen times last month and climaxed every time. That would shut down the beauty shop. Imagine.

Way too productive a day, by my standards. Drug out old fall decor and did 2 wreaths and Mama's cross for cemetery. Made a beef stew recipe from Southern Living. The house smells delish. Used wine for cooking. So not me, but I believe it will be good. Wes came to get Will and asked if I was okay. Everything is such an effort. So out of the habit.

Just enjoying the days I can and resting when I need to. As long as it's me dealing with things and nothing going on with the kids or Will.....I can deal. Glad I am lazy and easily satisfied. Realize it is a special gift God gave me. I am watching lots of older women torture themselves attempting to live up to cetain Southern standards. So glad I don't have any guilt about anything.

****

: Thankful for adult children who are kind, patient, and apparently still love their parents. So thankful for a large, very special extended family. Happy Thanksgiving to all my Facebook family and friends!

****

Love the tradition of posting words of thankfulness every day this month. Will start with one I have used before. November 1st is easy. Billy's birthday

****

Okay, so I cooked Billy a grand birthday breakfast. I gave him several cards. One mushy. One funny. And one truthful. We will celebrate tomorrow when I have an appointment in Montgomery. Made him three solemn promises.
1. No stopping at Costco.
2. No dropping me at the Casino.
3. And he can wear whatever he wants.

At my house, this is love and marriage. Happy Birthday, Billy Davis!

****

Thanks for all the likes and well wishes for Billy's birthday yesterday. Fun and flattering. One more time, Mama Mary was right. He does have nice manners and he was raised right. I love the way that my DNA and his DNA blended to make the best kids ever! Mama Mary did not venture into that area. Thank God!

****

If you don't understand the importance of coffee, just look at the mess I made trying to post early pictures and wish my husband a

Happy 69th Birthday. There are random pictures, double posts of the same things, and just a technological explosion of Billy Davis. Somewhat a model of our love and our marriage.....all over the place. Can't promise to improve. I love this man. He is a good man, a fun husband, a wonderful father to adult children, and Will's D. Once again in my life, I got way more than I deserved. Happy Birthday, Billy Davis!

****

I had a literal wake up call. The phone rang in the middle of the night last night. Made me think of all the people I love and care for and within five seconds, I worried about all of them. It was a wrong number! I am so very thankful for all of these people who instantly came to mind!

****

Thankful for blue sky at 11:11 on 11/11. Rather appropriate. Happy Veterans Day!

****

Thankful that I wake up happy nearly every morning. So glad I had a grandmother who spent her days smiling, whistling, and chuckling to herself. She taught me well.

****

I will vote today. Tonight I'll watch the election results, but first I will watch the BCS college football rankings on ESPN. Expect that it will be more fun.

****

Life is... Gratitude.

Thankful that We gather together to ask the Lord's blessing.... to quote an Old Methodist hymn that we were raised on. Boy, do we ever need it this year! Happy Thanksgiving!

****

I borrowed this picture from Kindal Maxey Burleson. I know she won't mind. The seated couple is Bily's aunt and uncle, Janie and Max Roberts. They are surrounded by three of their many grandchildren. Me Me and Pa Pa to these and many more.

We buried Billy's uncle about a week ago and his aunt will be laid to rest today. That, in itself, is a love story. We are Southerners and we know how to celebrate life. Billy's dad was an only child and his mom had two sisters. Billy and his sister Kay have only three first cousins. We would have to rent the coliseum if we combined both sides of my family.

Last night, we went to Montgomery for his aunt's visitation. We were invited to go back to her house on the east side of town for supper and family time. These cousins entertained exactly as I expected them to. They were raised right. We enjoyed a delicious meal. There was lots of laughter and hugs and a few tears.

When we were offered dessert, there was a pink cake which was part of a gender reveal party held a few days ago. Janie's youngest granddaughter is expecting a baby girl in a few months. I ate pink cake, and basked in the circle of life with my husband's extended

164

family. I felt the presence of his sweet Mother and his aunts and all the others who have gone before us. Life and death made sense for a few minutes on a quiet street in a brightly lit house with geraniums on the front porch. Family is everything!

****

I am thankful to live in a country that holds a special day of gratitude and thanksgiving. I am thrilled that the Thanksgiving holidays are difficult to commercialize and distort. I am grateful for abundance and traditions. My best memories and sweetest family recollections come from the Thanksgiving holidays. God Bless the USA. May we forever remain aware and appreciative.

****

Thanksgiving season is done. I won't be posting any more daily gratitude comments, BUT I will still be feeling it. Really got a boost out of giving my personal abundance deliberate thought and sharing those with you. Enjoy the rest of the holiday season with your family and friends.

****

I sure do enjoy fantasy living. Just not quite ready to go back to the routine. Have loved being able to tell my kids good night, face to face. Nothing sweeter than falling asleep hearing them laughing and talking together. Great for someone else to make the coffee and hang around to drink it with me. Marvelous to have a gourmet cook prepare beautiful meals. Thanksgiving has always been my favorite holiday. This was the best Thanksgiving ever. Counting my blessings.

Goodbye, November 2016! I have squeezed every bit of joy out of you. From November 1st, Billy's 70th birthday to November 30, one gigantic celebration. Glad you are not a 31 day month. My GI system could not have survived 24 more hours. Job well done.

Life is... Gratitude.

****

I have done a lot of deep thinking the past few days. So many on Facebook seem so clear about what they feel and what action should be taken by individuals and by our country. I do not have that clarity. Every time I think I might have made progress, I see the face of an innocent child on the news. There are no easy answers. God Bless the USA. God Bless the children.

"They are precious in his sight" as the old Sunday school song says.

****

June 21, 2001

Dear Julie,

Happy Birthday! I cannot believe that I have a 30-year-old child. I can think back and remember every tiny detail from the day you were born. Actually I can remember being pregnant and staying awake at night trying to imagine you. Even my imagination is not that good. The pre-sonogram days made everything a huge surprise. Those days were both scary and thrilling.

Sometimes I am afraid that we spend so much time reflecting on what a difficult child you were that I forget to tell you what wonderful joy motherhood has been. Within five minutes of your birth, I knew that I was fully capable of the grisly murder of anybody who dared to threaten my baby. The last 30 years have been a trial to keep those feelings under some semblance of control.

Even your most high maintenance day was a miracle to me. Daddy and I are so proud of you, your brilliant mind, your talents and triumphs, and your beautiful face. We could not be more elated to see the woman you have become. His nickname for you is perfectly apropos. "Flash" - you are the bright spark, the flame that reaches higher and burns more brilliantly. You have ignited your Mom on many occasions. Your enthusiasm has been the

Life is ... Common Ground

"lightard" for many. Your younger days cast me as an unwilling participant in a wild fire that no rainy day or roadblock could stop. Those teenage years are a bright red blur of activity, energy, and conflict. It was the ride of my life and except for a few photos and the scrapbooks, it seems like a dream or maybe a nightmare. If life is a journey then you dragged me, kicking and screaming, on the wildest roller coaster of all times. The dips and downs were the darkest and the heights were the tallest and wildest. It took my breath away and while I was hanging on for dear life, you were feeling the wind in your face and catching a glimpse of all the possibilities out there.

While our comfort levels will never merge and our interest levels will remain vastly different, I will always love you with a primitive fierceness that will never wane. My prayer was "God let her grow up and not need me so much." Now my prayer is "God let me grow old and not need her too much."

Happy Birthday to the most wonderful daughter in the world. Hope that this year will be the best yet. Wishing you a life that continues to be full of love and wonder. I will always be interested in the smallest trivial detail of your life. Having adult children has been a fantastic treasure to Daddy and me. Life is good!

I love you forever,

Mama

****

On April 26, 1976, I started believing in divine intervention. We lived out on the Troy Highway, in sight of the Pike County line. I was nine months pregnant. I hadn't seen my feet in months. We also had a female child who was almost five. She was known throughout the county as a wild child, who never slept and was as out of control as a feral cat. I was actually stopped on the sidewalks of Luverne when my pregnancy was showing and asked "WHY?" People could not believe we deliberately planned another one.

I had experienced a rocky pregnancy and was not well throughout

167

the entire process. We had foolishly chosen this time to remodel Billy's grandmother's country home. We had moved into the house in late March. On April 26, 41 years ago today, I shuffled into our little kitchen that used to be the back porch. When I stepped down, I hit a huge pool of water on the floor. I was sliding across the kitchen when Billy came in the back door and grabbed me in a bear hug before I hit the floor. The ice maker connection in our new refrigerator had broken and filled the room with water. We actually laughed. Billy turned off the water and mopped up the kitchen. No harm done.

The next day Wes was born in a scary emergency situation.

We both had an extremely close call. When Dr. Jim Alford, my obstetrician and a friend from the UAB days, came in to talk to us after all the drama settled, he said, "If you had fallen on that wet kitchen floor, you would have bled out within minutes." All this was due to a complicated condition that we didn't know about for my whole 9 months of pregnancy. There were no sonograms available in Montgomery at that time.

Due to a miracle, I have lived to be a mother, a teacher, and a grandmother. By the way, Julie became my closest friend and greatest gift. Wes is a doting son, who spoils his Mama in the best way. We won't even get into our grandson and the fun we have. I live in a state of gratitude and appreciation of my gift. Life is Good! I know exactly when God decided it was not my time to leave.

****

I didn't pack up this special ornament. This is our year! We will celebrate our 50th wedding anniversary in the summer. You know me! We'll celebrate all year long! It started with a beautiful engagement ring as my Christmas gift in 1967. Billy's parents hosted a Christmas open house and Billy chose that occasion to ask me to marry him in the presence of both sets of parents. He had the flu and was banished to his bedroom. I remember my Daddy standing as far away as possible and probably holding his breath.

Mama and Honey were already making lists before the ring was admired. I went back to Birmingham to finish the last semester of nursing school. I graduated in May, passed Boards in June, married in July, and was employed by the Health Department in August. And the rest is history. Billy had a year that he used to finish Troy State. We lived in Troy and had a year long honeymoon. I feel many more stories coming to the surface! Life is Good! Happy New Year!

Love is friendship that has caught fire. It is quiet understanding, mutual confidence, sharing and forgiving. It is loyalty through good and bad times. It settles for less than perfection and makes allowances for human weaknesses. - Ann Landers   Perfect quote to borrow for my husband's birthday. Happy 71st, Billy Davis! I love you too much! I was 20 when I made a commitment to you and suddenly it's 50 years later and it still stands! Life is Good!

Life is...
Fun!

Fairhope Adventure

We had a great day trip to Fairhope yesterday. I already over shared about that. There's an album recording the event. This is a whole nother deal.

I love random events that define us as a couple. We stopped at Publix in Daphne. We grabbed up some decadent items. Publix turns me into a kid in a candy store. The only healthy thing I put in my buggy was a pint of strawberries.

There were not a lot of checkouts open. I went to the 10 items or less line. Billy said I know we have more than ten items. He's always been a stickler for rules....Me...not so much. Also there are certain advantages to being gray-headed and crippled. I tote a bright blue cane, in case folks don't get it at first glance. Just to be fair, I did let a woman with two items go ahead of me.

As we piled our slightly more than ten items on the counter, a young woman stepped up behind me. She pointed to a pack of bakery cupcakes I had just unloaded. "What you got going on there?" I replied, "I think they call them wedding cupcakes." The chatty young woman said, "I've got some chicken necks and I'm fixing to go feed an alligator. Wanna come?" I take great pride in being the type person who gets invited to a wild gator feeding.

Billy had been loading groceries and dealing with the credit card. He hadn't heard any of my conversation with the gator lady. I told him all about it as he grumbled about getting everything into our small cooler.

The gator lady waved at me in the parking lot like a long lost friend and shouted "Come on and join me. It's right behind the store. It'll be fun." I turned to Billy and said, "Let's go!" Billy smiled and said "Why not?" I wondered if this was a set up. I was thinking that it sounds like something you see on Dateline. Elderly couple lured from Publix parking lot with the promise of a gator feeding. Their abandoned car found with a load of fattening food and a blue cane.

We easily located a beautiful park overlooking the Bay. I spotted the gator lady at the end of the pier tossing chicken necks into the water. Joining her would have involved a very long walk out to the end of the pier. I wasn't up to the trek, but it was great that we checked it out. As we pulled away, I told Billy that I am so glad I married a man who didn't turn down adventures.

We headed to the Causeway just because I love that route. I also like crossing the huge double bridges that truckers call the Dolly Partons. We had a really fun day. We've had nearly 50 years of fun days.

****

We had a hot date last night. We ate Chinese takeout in the car while listening to an audio book. We were parked in our own back yard. We stayed out til 9:30. I love growing old together.

****

Brantley, you had a beautiful prom last night. Luverne, I know your prom will be wonderful tonight, in spite of a vicious storm and power outages that lasted several days. I realize that these young people do not read Facebook posts from old ladies. I know some of your parents, grandparents, and even great grandparents do.

Back in the day, we had the Junior - Senior Banquet, the L Club Banquet, and the Band Banquet. All these events were dressy affairs with seated meals and dates. The meal for Junior - Senior Banquet was limited to only 11th and 12th graders. As strange as it sounds, you often had one date for the meal and another date for the dance. Planning was as complex as political strategy. It often involved the whole family. I remember that L Club was held during the Christmas Season. I recall a huge cedar tree cut from some local forest. It was sprayed with silvery paint and touched the ceiling of the auditorium. The L Club was limited to guys who lettered at football and the varsity cheerleaders. Very exclusive and a date to this event was quite coveted.

The Junior - Senior Banquet was also a big deal. The theme was a well kept secret. We spent many days ahead preparing and decorating. The Junior Class hosted the Seniors. There was entertainment and place cards and a printed menu with cleverly worded descriptions of dry chicken and green beans. Who ate anyway? The dance was a combination of crepe paper, mirror balls, and sometimes a real fountain rigged up by Ag classes around some little sister's inflated swimming pool. But at night with a frothy dress and fresh flowers worn on the wrist......it became truthfully magical.

There will be some sweet memories made this weekend. Cherish these times, pretty people. Also know the best is yet to be!

Happy Valentines to Mama in Heaven! Just so you know, your children love each other. We have not had a single cross word or an argument, fuss, or fight since you left us in 2007. Sorry that we fought like thugs when we were kids. Guess we got over it! We love you!

****

I remember sitting on the hood of a Jeep in the Homecoming Parade with Annette Mitchell Sikes. We were little girls, dressed in matching outfits. I remember we wore white vinyl jackets and knitted caps and gloves I think I remember seeing a picture of us. We had a sign that said Class of '6? I think somebody did the math wrong. Pretty sure it didn't say Class of '65, but the number seemed so far away.

When I was about 10, we had homecoming queens who were beautiful twins. Sylvia and Sybil Smith were stunning in matching blue formals. It was very unusual for the queen to wear any color other than our school colors. Of course, we'd never had two queens and it was just fine for them to be in blue. I can remember exactly where the float was parked and exactly how stunning they were. I was in awe.

Been thinking about Luverne Homecoming all afternoon. Things are so different now, but I wanted to share how it used to be. There is no way to total the hours that I was out of class due to crepe paper and/or tissue paper. I carried a good pair of sharp scissors every where. If I could get a teacher to write me a pass to help decorate a float, the gym, or make streamers for the goal posts, I was in heaven. Broke my heart when I heard that school supply companies started selling rolls of precut streamers. So glad I was in college when that catastrophe occured.

Also remember that cheerleaders made their own shakers. Now I think they are called pom poms. I know they are metallic and indestructible. In the 50's and 60's, it took hours to make them from tissue paper. I made my own the one year I was a "B" Team cheerleader. The cheerleaders kept plastic bags nearby. If there was a drop of rain, they had to quickly stuff them in the bags or the paper would melt away.

I cut crepe paper for the goal posts. We all thought that was a beautiful way to decorate. It had to be done after the pep rally on Friday afternoon. They wouldn't last long. I remember getting chill bumps when the band would play the Fight Song and the Luverne Tigers would run through our specially cut crepe paper streamers. Nothing better. Enjoy Homecoming on Friday. Make your own memories. Life is Good! Go Tigers!

****

I have a long list of movies I won't watch. Anything about zombies, vampires, werewolves, blood suckers....no matter how handsome the actors are....is not happening with me. When Will was a toddler, who never napped, never had a pacifier, was basically a free range chicken, I would allow anything in the DVD player to get through the long afternoons. I was retired and the parents, the other grandparents, and everybody else was working. It was up to me.

One afternoon, Will put on Dodgeball and I let it play. He loved when one player would decimate another with the ball. If the ball flipped them over backwards and made a nose bleed, he would clap his little hands and belly laugh. Great fun! I noticed that it gave me a headache and I started to sweat. Wes came in from work and laughed at what Will had conned me into watching. Will promptly said, "Bye, Ya Ya." I was free to go.

When I got home and watered my plants and enjoyed the quiet, it came rushing back to me where my strange reaction to this silly movie had come from. Margaret Spurlock Ballard. When she was a senior and I was a 7th grader at Luverne High School, there was a period of time when we were scheduled for girls PE class together. Here I was introduced to dodge ball at a whole new level. I had played at recess on the playground at the elementary school. There it was a harmless game with giggles and grins. Not so in the gym. I was never lucky enough to get picked for Margaret's team. I can picture myself with my white, spindly legs in that atrocious bubble suit. Fresh meat! Margaret was a powerful warrior, who was born generations too soon. I can imagine her in today's world with all the athletics for female students. She was awesome! On the days when we walked into the gym and I spotted the soft dodgeballs on the shiny floor, I knew I was bound to be an early casualty. I really tried hard, but it was going to happen. I just tried to protect my nose and my teeth. My pride was not even a consideration. She would set her powerful legs and launch that ball with undeniable accuracy. It was then a matter of when, not if. It was a relief to be sent to the wall and to rest my back on the cool bricks after receiving the disqualifying hit. Then I could openly cheer for my team, against Margaret, but not loud enough for her to take it personally.....just in case there was time for a second match.

Through the miracle of Facebook, Margaret and I are friends. We message each other several times a week. She still amazes me. She is a survivor. She has lost a child and a spouse. Margaret will always be a warrior in my eyes. She is a hard worker with many skills. She's recently been sick and been to the doctor, which is apparently a rare occurrence. Thank you, Margaret Spurlock Ballard, for allowing me to tell my little story. You have impressed me! Life is Good!

Life is ... Common Ground

****

Beautiful dawn celebration. Already planning for next year. We missed you, Carolyn Knox Lynn, celebrating World Naked Gardening Day - 2017.

****

I promise I am not being one bit morbid and no, I don't have a premonition, but when I go and if you decide to come to my memorial service, I have several suggestions.

First. Bring a newspaper. Hope things won't be so boring that you need reading material. I want you to line your trunk or back seat with that newspaper. Please do not send flowers when I go. We are going to reverse that tradition. I have a plan that involves leaving Billy plant free. At the moment I figure I have maybe 200 containers, filled with growing plants. Billy tolerates these because they make me very happy.

I think that Wes, Will and a posse of my favorite nephews can fill a flatbed trailer with my garden. It may take a police escort to ease this plant-mobile out to Emmaus Cemetery from the Airport Road, but it can be done. Conveniently our plot is located at the very backside of the cemetery. There is room for a truck and trailer. I promise that the service will be short and sweet. There will be music. Some of my grads have pledged to handle that. Once the service is complete, my friends and fellow gardeners can claim a plant or two. See I have thought this thing out.

Billy will then only need to feed some birds and maybe fill a hummingbird feeder or not. Thank you, in advance, for your cooperation. I am a planner and a list maker. I feel better now.

****

Happy February, Facebook Friends and Family! This is my favorite month. This is the love month and this is my birthday month. Wait, wait.....don't wish me Happy Birthday yet! I'm not ready! I turn 70 on February 23rd. I am going to milk this month to the max.

Life is... Fun!

We are going to celebrate Valentines Day first. We don't get all that excited about Ground Hog Day and we are lukewarm about Presidents Day!

Also I need to mention that if you begin to be burned out with all my posts and pictures, use the unfollow feature. It won't hurt my feelings and it will give you a break. Happy February!

Yesterday was definitely the calm after the storm. The sun was shining brightly. There was a chilly breeze, but not more than a light jacket could handle. Coffee was hot and perfect. My knees were not so good. I was hobbling around like Festus on Gunsmoke. Since Billy was working, I made the decision to loll in bed with a good book and my microwave hot packs. And then there was a knock at the back door. My partner in crime had different ideas. Donny Ray Holmes was on his way to the library. "Stick on some clothes and we'll run down to 106 when I get back. You don't have to walk. You can just point." He knew just how to dangle the carrot in front of the old gray mare.

We had the best time. Beautiful ride down to Jean's Garden. We were the only patrons. School and work had resumed in town. DR set me up in a lawn chair right in the middle of the gorgeous array of flowers and plants. Two ladies were arranging a new plant shipment. The husband of one of the workers was rocking his fussy grandbaby while a rolly polly puppy played at his feet. When he started singing a sweet lullaby, I wondered if I had died and gone to Heaven.

We filled up the back of my vehicle with a floral rainbow. After a quick stop to pick up lunch, we went home to the Airport Road. My biggest problem Thursday afternoon was making the potting soil, the plants, and the pots come out even. What a wonderful problem to have!

Donny Ray and I laughed and talked the day away. We were both up to our elbows in potting soil. We have our health issues, but this special day we shoved them into a back corner. Plant therapy is my favorite remedy. We were still at it when Billy came home. He was appropriately impressed. He knows what makes me happy.

Everybody needs a hobby, a friend, and a few special spring days. I know I paint a pretty picture of retirement and aging. Who wants to read about dark days anyway? It is the truth when I say Life is Good!

****

In my dreams...Kentucky Derby Day! I bought this to annoy my kids. Have to use it once in a while. The closest I'll be to a horse is the equine manure Donny Ray uses for my flowers. And there is the Crenshaw County Rodeo next door at the Ag Center. Life is Good! — at Kentucky Derby.

Life is... Fun!

Since today is Siblings Day I decided to share an unusual Perdue story.

When I was about 19 years old and attending University Hospital School of Nursing in Birmingham, my parents decided to have me declared an adult by court order. I would become an "emancipated minor". Their master plan was if they died in an accident, I would be responsible for rearing my three younger brothers. If I were 19, that meant that Bob would have been 17, Jim 14 1/2, and Tom 12. I cannot imagine a bigger train wreck. I still don't know what possessed our parents to dream this up. I am positive that they didn't have a drinking problem.

The most fun thing to come out of this was that I was served legal papers by a deputy sheriff in full uniform, including a gun and a shiny badge, inside University Hospital. This process was observed by a number of curious classmates and some of the hospital staff. Since I was not carried away in handcuffs, I was just considered a questionable character for a few days. In fact, I do believe that was the year I was selected as Class Favorite. I am glad that both my parents lived many, many more years and that I never became responsible for my siblings.

We lived happily ever after and I am not certain that I ever became a real adult. Now you know the rest of the story.

****

Sue McDougald Watson just made me remember a funny. I am so obsessed with my BIG birthday coming up. I told Billy that once I hit 70, it's all going to be about me and I am not going to do anything I don't really want to do.

Billy smirked at me and commented "And that would be different how?" I laughed and snorted tea through my nose

****

Happy Valentines Day! I have gotten hugs and kisses, some a little early, from my main man, our daughter, our son, and our grandson. Also cards, candy, gifts, and flowers have arrived.

When we moved to the Airport Road, Wes and Will dug up all my special daffodil bulbs and planted them in my new yard. The bulbs were a gift from our niece, Stephanie G Cornett. Yes, you can measure love. I can see these from my kitchen window. So special!

****

April Fools' Day. I really miss my Daddy today. He was a renowned prankster and he loved this day! Every joke he played.....I fell for - hook. line, and sinker.

One year he really got Mama. He had warned her repeatedly that she needed to stop running into local stores and grabbing items without asking the price. Back in the day, most families had accounts in every downtown store. Accounts were normally settled up at the end of the month. Daddy plotted and planned with the local hardware store. I think Mr. Henry Hilburn was in on this one.

Mama was in the middle of a project and ran in, grabbed a simple paint brush, and popped back home. In a few weeks, on April 1, Daddy presented her with the hardware bill. There had been a fake bill created. One paintbrush was listed as being priced at $25. You could probably have fed a family for a week on that amount.

I think Mama managed to hide her shock. Imagine Daddy was smirking right over her shoulder. When she called the hardware, as part of the setup, she was told that the bristles were imported from France and the handle made about some very rare and expensive wood. I know she was thinking that her four kids were going to eat bologna for the entire month of April. Daddy went even further and appeared to be going through the bills. He pitched a fit when he got to the hardware and just about the time Mama teared up, he shouted, " April Fools!"

She was so relieved that I don't think she even got mad. She was quite happy to pay for the $1.25 paintbrush and move on. The people and the things that we miss! April Fools', Daddy Guy!

****

Thank you, Janice Hall, for my surprise. You are a good, good friend. Slow down long enough next time to drink some coffee from the Life is Good cup you gave me. Love you!

****

Mothers Day Month. I miss my Mama. I do not miss what dementia did to her. I do miss having a strong, scary, clever mother. I miss Mary Perdue being smartest woman in the room. I miss her love that was seldom stated, but demonstrated daily. I miss her aggravating independence. I do not miss her loud mouth and the words she screamed at the referees at Luverne High School football games. Bursting into an impromptu tap dance at a public gathering is cute.....when the performer is not YOUR mother.

I miss Mama being a Rambo grandma to eight Perdue grands. I am glad she got to know the only great grandchild born before her death. And yes, I do ride out to the cemetery and talk to her a couple of times a month. It does not upset me, but it doesn't comfort me that much either. I take a little whisk broom and clean off her military marker. Sometimes I stay a little while and always drive by Daddy, my grandparents, my beloved aunt, Judy, and nod to my great grandparents I never knew.

Family is everything. I look forward to reading and hearing all the tributes to mothers. This is a special month, but nothing is more special than the mothers who make us who we are. Thanks, Mama. Rest in peace!

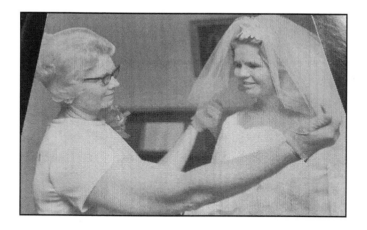

****

This little post is directed at you young, pretty people who have recently been to prom or are planning a beach trip or maybe really enjoy passing near a mirror. Things will change. Just want you to know that getting older is okay, too. It can even be fun. I still wake up and look forward to my day. I laugh a lot more than I cry.

Keep your passions, your dreams, and your sense of humor. Getting old is a privilege. Find folks to love. Find something that you like to do. Never lose yourself in the struggle. Life is Good! I promise.

****

Life is... Fun!

Billy's mother always used these little white ceramic cupids with her Valentines centerpieces. She was a wonderful cook and she set a beautiful table with live flowers, linen tablecloths and napkins and her real silver serving pieces. This was one of her special things I received after her death.

Tonight I looked at the base in a bright light. The faded tag read Woolworth $2.99. I beg to differ. Priceless!

****

It's a sure thing that you're getting old when you start to get nostalgic about foolish things. Mama did not have a green thumb. She had a few things that grew in spite of her. Mama had a line of nandina bushes that grew on the north end of the big house. The bushes thrived in their location. I'm pretty sure that my parents' landscaping plan had to do with a busted crate of starter shrubs that Mr. Howard Morgan gave them. They just stuck them in the ground in the late 60s when the house was completed. I'm pretty certain the nandinas were planted without any special consideration or thought. Most years there was a huge crop of nandina berries which were usually orange by Thanksgiving and bright red by Christmas. I enjoyed using them during the holidays.

186

Life is ... Common Ground

When Wes moved to the big house, he and Will moved my knock out roses and my daffodils to the Airport Road. Wes completely cleared out the nandinas. He has cut out lots of box wood and shrubs that had taken over the yard. He used Roundup liberally. Now it is very open and well groomed. He is a lawn man.

The other afternoon when I took Will home after school. I noticed a tiny nandina seedling that had popped up in the spot that had once been thick with the plants. When Will went inside, I hobbled around to the side of the house and was able to ease the plant out of the loose soil. I took it to our house. The very next day, Wes brought me some old pots that he found clearing up around Mama Mary's little house on Third Street in town. Inside there was a small nandina along with some thriving poison ivy and an army of fireants.

The next morning Billy dug two holes on the north side of the Airport Road house. I now have a nandina from the big house on the farm and I have another nandina from the house that was Mama's last house on this earth. And I have another story. Wonder if I'll have berries by the holidays? Nothing wrong with a little nostalgia.

****

Life is... Fun!

I am so spoiled. Got this beautiful early birthday cake today as a surprise from Roslyn Brown. Just on the way to cut it and have some hot tea and my favorite Key Lime cake.

When Roslyn and Richard were dating, they used to play monopoly with me on the living room rug at her sister's (Sara Bond) apartment on Glenwood Ave. They were the most gorgeous couple. Still are! We lived across the street in the house where Betty Pippin lives now.

Those were some of the best times. I'm sure I was a pesky kid, but both of them were so sweet to me. Thank you, Roslyn, for such a wonderful birthday gift.

****

If you see my husband, Billy, in town today, please do not ask him what is wrong. Please! This is completely out of my control. Dale Earnhardt Jr. announced his retirement this afternoon. This will so test our relationship. Losing Dale Earnhardt Sr was a major trial for us, but this is very serious business.

We are much older. We as a couple are in a delicate condition. We will celebrate our 50th wedding anniversary next summer....if we can make it through this roadblock. I am seriously considering having #88 tattooed in some meaningful location just to demonstrate my sympathy and understanding.

Thank you for your love and support. Life must go on!

****

A perfect Spring Monday. Birds are singing. Bees are buzzing. Butterflies flitting from bloom to bloom. A Mama bird has a worm in her beak, headed to a nest. A single hummingbird is at my front feeder. No one looking for a fight.

Everything is made sweeter by the laughter of children at the Ag Center for a school event. Peace and serenity waft in like a sweet, dense fog. Sitting and reflecting work. You can't chase happiness.

****

We lost our Aunt Helen Bailey, Mama Mary's sister, three years ago today. She spoiled me rotten. I was such a shy, retiring child, but she brought me right out of that. Will always love her and her kids, Ann Bailey and Jack Bailey. Will miss her daughter, Elaine, who left us way too soon. Nothing like family.

Life is... Fun!

****

April 1st has been a gorgeous day, so why was I sitting on my back deck pouting like a 1st grader? I had a golf cart filled with beautiful plants and flowers from Jean's on 106. I had all day to do what I love to do.....put my hands in rich, dark potting soil and make things happen. Sounds great, but I admit I was stewing over age, arthritis, and aches and pains. After finally completing two or three small pots, I realized it might be Halloween by the time that I realistically could get finished. Maybe it was about time to throw in the gardening towel or trowel and just give it up.

I heard a vehicle turn in the driveway. It was my son. Wes had been working for several days grooming the schools and getting things ready for spring. He said, "I'm all yours." I made a token attempt to insist that he go home and get his shower and maybe a nap. He said I haven't seen you all week. I'm in no rush.

I do mean it when I say... Yes, you can measure love. All my pots are now planted, watered and the deck is neat and clean. My spirits are lifted as high as the blue spring sky. No way for Wes to really know how happy he made his Mama. He said he likes it when I cry for happy reasons. Life is Good!

Life is...
Later.

Bras on the Lawn Chairs

I read that we only made the Top 100 Redneck Cities in Alabama. I am doing what I can to elevate our standing.

Yesterday I hung my Sunday bra out to dry on a lawn chair. Made sense to place this chair smack dab in the middle of our paved driveway. That hard rain came up and about 15 minutes later I remembered the laundry item.

That bra had soaked up so much rain water that it tipped the chair over backwards. Might I mention that I had on pajamas at five o'clock in the afternoon when I retrieved the lingerie from the yard.

One woman can only do so much single handedly to raise our status. Come on girls! Let your country show! Life is Good!

Napping Outside

Took a nap outside sitting up straight in a dusty lawn chair. Was sure hoping some pretty little fairies would flit around me and work some magic. Flat sho didn't happen. Think I did snort down a gnat or two.

Winter was so mild that it looks this pretty before anything gets done. If I get out and fall, it will mess up Billy and Dr. Pat's spring fishing plans. I have to behave or else.

Billy foolishly suggested that I ride down to Jean's on 106 just to look. Might as well hire a drunk as a bartender. I just got buzzed by a fairy or possibly an early hummingbird. Stay tuned.

****

The Real "F" Words

Billy is working today. He had to go to bed early. I left the Texas A & M/Duke score for him on a little note by the coffee maker!

He is not a Johnny Manziel fan and he wrote back "Dog gone it!" He promises that he will be home on Monday night!

I am all about the F words - family, football, food, fun! Got ya!

****

The beauty of what used to be called a weed. We could learn so much from nature if we would.

Interesting story with this particular lantana. Wes was mowing and snagged a broken piece of one of the lantanas at the back of the yard. The mower dropped this little limb. Wes forgot to go back and pick it up from the corner of the house. Next time he noticed, it had taken root. This beautiful bush was not deliberately planted, was never fertilized or watered. It is an unplanned treasure.

****

We rode to Troy today to Douglas Brothers to get my rings cleaned. I told Billy that was all I really needed for our upcoming anniversary. He said that would be great because he was trying to think of something to do for me.

We dropped the rings off and went to lunch and then to make life complete, I got a dipped DQ cone for dessert. Went back to pick up the sparkling rings and there was no charge for the cleaning. We both laughed big.

Life is ... Common Ground

Sometimes life is just too simple.

Reflecting on Happiness

At 70 I do a lot of reflecting. Summers have always been my favorite time. As a kid, I don't remember ever being bored. Mama believed strongly in child labor. She was a renowned list maker. She had a chore list on her special family blackboard and she kept it filled. The first name on her work assignment list was always Pat, written in Mama's pretty script. My chores were doable, but also undeniable. It never crossed my mind to skip an assignment. I remember the wonderful feeling of having completed my chores and being free for the rest of the day.

I have somewhat reached that plateau in my life. Physically I am limited, but emotionally I am as free as a bird. I like this picture of myself. Probably the last time I dipped my nicely manicured toes into warm, salt water at the coast. Billy let me use his arm to hobble down under the Destin Bridge. Then he stepped back and made this picture.

We have the very best time when we go to the beach. Now beach time involves riding and plundering around some of our favorite spots and discovering new places. It does not involve much walking. Thank goodness I love people watching, balcony sitting and reading.

Do not feel sorry for me. I have as much fun now as I did when I was a kid. I like being known as the Life is Good lady. Happiness is a choice.

****
Cropping – a Super Power

This phone has a feature that has pretty much changed my life. It has to do with the built in camera, but I am using this skill throughout my life. It's called cropping. Don't laugh now! Really.

For example, yesterday I hobbled out to my nifty golf cart. I drove all around the yard making pictures of the plants that made it through our mild winter. When I got safely back inside, I sat down and cropped out the weeds, the dead limbs, the mess. I confess that I do this all the time. When I have some part of my life that's bugging me, I crop it! When I realize something is stealing my joy, I crop it. When I notice crumbs, wrinkles, dust in a picture, crop it! When I drag out an old family picture with a person who is no longer legally related to me.....crop. Most importantly, I crop out my crippled leg, my frowns, my negative issues....all the bad stuff, gone.

Last week a young mother commented to me that she thought my life was perfect. I hugged her and laughed. I just have a super power and it's called cropping. Have a good Sunday!

****

I may have carried this retired and relaxed life style just a tad too far. This morning when Wes came to pick up Will after breakfast,

he asked "Why are you so dressed up, Mama?"
I had on jeans, a tee shirt, and some mascara! LOL!

****

Passion in Marriage

We have an anniversary coming up next month. We have been a couple for nearly half a century. I want to say a little something about passion. Don't panic, Julie, Wes, and all my adult nieces and nephews. I am not talking about "sex" on Facebook. Relax!

One definition of passion is "a strong and barely controllable emotion". Please don't think that every nice post I write about Billy Davis means that he is always sweet, patient, and easy going. Oh, no.

Just so you know, we had a passionate incident in the garage on Friday morning that would rapidly erase any of those ideas. Not that it matters, but the subject under discussion was the temperature setting on the air conditioning thermostat. Our volume cleared all wildlife from the yard. I think a few cars on the Airport Road may have been put in reverse, in order to rapidly exit the battleground. There was no bloodshed. There was profanity. We were both mad, really mad.

A person cannot reach that level of anger without passion. I did not imagine this scene when I wore white in the candle lit sanctuary of the Luverne Methodist Church in 1968. The preacher, Bro. John Vickers, did mention it in our vows. He wasn't kidding about the better or worse and sickness or health parts. I was so focused on finally getting to go to the beach for a week without my mother that I didn't pay attention.

We got over this "fuss". Billy went to town to drink coffee with some other old guys. When he came back home, the first thing he said was "I'm sorry." It wasn't even his fault.

We let off some steam and this has been a stressful week. Later in the day we went to town for ice cream and held hands while we rode out to the Crenshaw County Lake.

Life is... Later.

This is what passion is to me. Certainly not a life that looks like the cover of a paperback romance novel. It's real people living real lives.

****

My husband has been down in the back, BUT he is headed out to attempt to mow the yard. My knees are not cooperating, BUT I am going to water my plants.

This is sort of the theme of our married life. Keep on keeping on! Soon be 46 years. We are plodders and Life is Good!

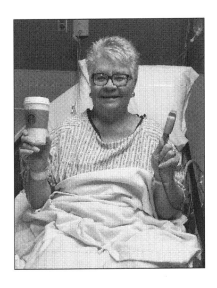

Elderly, Obese White Female

No worries. This picture is about 8 months ago. My point in posting this again is to let my Facebook friends know I am a tough old bird. When I was wheeled from the heart cath lab to recovery, the tech plopped my chart down in my lap. In the old days, the medical chart was guarded as if it were a treasure map to a trunk of gold coins. That particular morning, as soon as I was given my glasses, I read the first line on the front page of my chart. ELDERLY,

OBESE WHITE FEMALE. It's a wonder they didn't have to deal with cardiac arrest. Not a single mention of great sense of humor, looks good in purple, thick hair. I'm Southern, for Pete's sake! Break it to me gently. We all know the rules.

Anyway today is special. I've had a fabulous birthday month. I have enjoyed some big time spoiling from my loving family. Really, I wouldn't change a thing.

****

Water pressure fine on Airport Road. Not using mine til 2:17. Just enough time to rinse off and get to LHS for the dismissal bell.

Do not come to see me today. If you're selling, I'm not buying. If you haven't seen me in a while, you can wait another day or two.

If you are kin to me, you know better.

****

Monumental day of extreme separation. We were so emotionally attached, but the time came for change.

Yes, you guessed it. We have purged two refrigerators. We have eggs, milk, and some assorted salad dressing. Everything else was moldy, spoiled, or out of date. Some items could only have been identified in one of those labs we see on crime shows.

Definite progress has been made. Our goals achieved. Life is Good! Happy New Year!

****

Men's Health Issues

I hereby volunteer to serve on a State Committee that will obviously soon be formed to make important decisions concerning male health issues.

I am highly qualified since I grew up in a home with three brothers. I am a Registered Nurse. I have been married to the same man for 45 years and I have a son and a grandson.

Since men seem to consider themselves highly qualified to make health decisions for women of all ages, please turn me loose. I am ready, willing, and able!

Sometimes the strangest things happen that let me know that my husband really loves me. Billy Davis hates sweet potato vines. He says they are nothing but kudzu. He thinks snakes love to hide beneath them. He asks me every spring to not plant them, but I must.

The other day as he mowed the lawn, I glanced out of the kitchen window and saw him gently move a long tendril of my sweet potato vine and place it out of the reach of the lawn mower blades.

I smiled as my heart did that special marital bump, as he renewed our vows...one more time!

****

This has been a special day for me. Ten years ago I tried my first day of retirement when the other teachers went back to work and I stayed home. I was retired all summer, but I didn't feel retired because all the other teachers were on vacation, too. Suddenly it was just me and free time.

I started keeping a journal that very first day on August 9, 2005. Since then I have documented the deaths of both my parents, deaths of friends, many marriages, just about as many divorces, and of course illnesses, surgeries, and all that jazz. Primarily I recorded the mundane daily trivial details of life in a small Southern town. I have never been bored. I love nature. I love flowers and plants. I love being a wife, a mother, and a grandmother. I love to read. My life is pretty simple, but I find lots to laugh about. Mostly I laugh at myself.

Pat Davis is content. My bucket list is short.

****

Blotting Pizza

I saw a hint about eating pizza as I watched the Today Show earlier in the week. That little Barbie doll person who talks about nutrition suggested that you take a paper napkin and blot your slice of pizza before you eat it. Understand that I buy lean ground beef. I blot bacon with a paper towel before I serve it in my own home. I make homemade soup and I chill it in order to remove extra fat before eating it. I do not fry food inside my kitchen. Ever. Billy fries fish outside in a pot when/if he ever catches enough to cook.

BUT if you blot a slice of pizza at a restaurant while dining with me...... prepare yourself to immediately lose your dining companion.

You have been warned. Life is Good, but I am not that good.

****

It's been exactly a year ago today since I started my quest to get something done about my knees. I met my orthopedic surgeon in Dothan, with the plan to eventually have surgery at Hughston Clinic in Columbus, Georgia. I was presented with a thick packet of pre-op forms and a required procedures check list. And we started this journey after being asked if I had a living will. I do have a living will, but this somehow felt like getting divorce forms when one goes to the courthouse for a marriage license.

I am going to keep this to a reasonable length. I have had two sets of X-rays, an MRI, lab work, and now the heart cath. And I have developed a neck issue that has far surpassed the knee problems in the areas of pain and discomfort. That neck, jaw, shoulder pain and an inconclusive EKG led to postponement of my scheduled orthopedic surgery.

In preparation for our trip to Montgomery for possible cardiac issues, I suggested to Billy that we go to the safe deposit box at our local bank and retrieve my living will. He thought I was being dramatic, but he went along with it. As we sat at the kitchen table sorting through numerous medical forms, Wes dropped by. He was lamenting the fact that he had been out begging for money for the Luverne High School Marching Band's upcoming fall season. I commented that if I passed away during any of my upcoming medical procedures that his Daddy could forgo floral tributes and request donations be made to the Band. My son and my husband failed to see the humor in this while I thought it was a viable solution for meeting the financial needs of the band.

I had so many medical forms that I actually resorted to using my SEC football clipboard to hold them all. We made our preparations for the Thursday trip for the heart cath. The very worst part of a medical procedure is definitely starting a day without coffee. I made the hour drive to Montgomery with my eyes closed due to the horrible caffeine headache that jumped on me about 5:30 a.m.

I am not certain, but I think when we pulled up to valet parking that the attendant asked "Do you have a living will?" When I met with the admission clerk in the cath lab, she asked for my insurance cards and then asked. "Do you have a living will?" I was prepared and pulled that thing from my football clipboard and she made a copy. I didn't even say "I told you so" to my spouse. I just gave him that look.

When I entered the cubicle and surrendered my clothes to the nurse and received that attractive hospital gown.....yep, you guessed it... Do you have a living will?

When I was finally rolled back for the heart cath, Billy kissed me and whispered in my ear "No fundraising for the Band today. Got that?" Always something to laugh about. Life is Good! Do you have a living will?

****

Free Advice Friday. People often ask what is the secret to having a long marriage. Simple. Neither of us ever left the other one. Guaranteed to be successful. Also helps to laugh a lot.

****

I try not to bother Facebook with my whining, but tonight...I just feel the need. I caught Billy's cold. This time I decided to deal with it just like a man. I haven't moved all day. As my Mamaw used to describe it, I haven't hit a lick at a snake. 8 o'clock and here I recline in the same pajamas I woke up in. I really pushed myself midday and thawed some camp stew. I have moved just enough not to develop a blood clot. I'll continue this story tomorrow if you can handle the excitement. Snort, snort. Good night!

****

Last night just when I was ready to turn off the bedroom lamp, I asked Billy "Did you turn off that sprinkler? " His response "Do you still have on shoes?" I will translate this for you single folks. YOU do it! Sooooo I had the opportunity to enjoy the cool night air and the chirp of crickets. Marriage is not always 50/50. You newlyweds with all these beautiful photos on Facebook should also take heed. Life is Good, but not always fair.

****

How to Sex Chickens

The Chicken Chick®: How to Sex Chickens: Male or Female, Hen or Rooster? (www.the-chicken-chick.com)

I simply asked Billy how to tell if a young chicken was male or female. This sudden interest was "egged" on by seeing the runaway chicken in front of the Chicken Shack. I am easily entertained. The Internet informed me that sexing chicken is a rare skill. Sooooo glad my husband was a farmer/truck driver and not a chicken sexer. Can you imagine?

My Thoughts on a Local Funeral

Had to eat some words or at least, gag on some thoughts Sunday afternoon. The funeral was an eye-opener for Billy and me. Deceased had experienced a turn around several years ago. Had stopped drinking and he had been teaching Sunday school for the past two years at a small church in Luverne. The two ministers who did the service were both in tears and his wife and two young children were obviously distraught. His wife kept leaning over the casket to stroke that straggly gray hair as if there wasn't one weird thing about him. Don't know many folks our age who could have been sent off any better. It should remind me that you never really know another person, even in Luverne where we are right up under each other. Have thought about ***** all week. I plan to learn from this.

On Becoming 70

When one becomes 70, you are always looking for something....always. I don't remember what I was searching for, but I am thrilled with what I found. I do not remember being the mother who bought these matching outfits. I don't recall making ponytails and tying color coordinated hair bows. It's all a blur, all the shoe fittings, the trips to Montgomery, the budgets and the bills. Suddenly I'm an old lady with adult children who take me to fancy dinners with delicious food. They pick up the check. They drive to the restaurant door to drop me off and pick me up. They say "Watch your step, Be careful, Do you need the restroom?"

Where did that young woman go and where in the world did this old lady come from? Glad I found pictures I wasn't looking for.

Day Beach Trip

Just got home from a week at the beach. Brought back lots of childhood memories as I sat on the balcony and watched the world go by.

Mama Mary often took the four of us alone and on a limited budget. We packed for ourselves. Fashion was not a consideration. Swimsuits for my brothers were most likely cutoff jeans. I usually had a hand-me-down, faded one piece swimsuit from my cousin,

Life is... Later.

Nancy Watts. I was proud to get it, too.

We went to the public beach. I recall that there were no beach toys, colorful towels, or sunscreen. We went early and were sent to the shade when the sun got too strong. My Daddy thought sunburns were a sign of bad parenting.

We did take a big truck tire tube. It had a sharp valve stem that blessed the user with a long red scratch on the inner thigh. It was worth it. Almost a badge of honor.

We knew about undertow, jellyfish, and just how much sand could work its way into the seams of our beach wear.

The beach was a magical place where rich people lived. We knew a day trip was a wonderful gift. We were blessed with a great childhood. I think those trips were very important. Almost Christmas in July.

****

Ate my camp stew for lunch. Wanted to share the story, as I remember it, of camp stew making at Luverne School. Pretty sure stew was made for Homecoming and for the Halloween Carnival. Each classroom was responsible for a recipe or a making. I can see the ingredients list on the big blackboards. "5 lb.Bag of Onions. 10 lb. Bag of Irish Potatoes. Canned tomatoes. Bottle of catsup."

I do not remember the pork and beef listed, but I do remember two hens. I remember kids bringing food from home. The farm kids brought chickens from their own backyards. I know they brought those hens wrapped in paper bags on the school buses.

I never saw anything in an ice chest. I don't remember ice chests and I don't remember food poisoning. I can see the lunch room ladies and some of the mothers peeling potatoes and cutting up onions. I see the dads and some of the coaches standing around open fires and huge black iron pots. They stirred with wooden boat paddles. When the cooking process started, the early smells were not that pleasant. Later in the day, as the stew cooked down and the foods blended in the pots, the delicious aroma surrounded the school. It was an exciting time for all the kids. I am recalling the 50's and early 60's. Anything out of the ordinary was thrilling. I

206

love camp stew. The memories are more wonderful than the food. I so hope the children of today are making a few memories that have nothing to do with technology. We have our homemade ice cream, our stalks of sugar cane, and our camp stew cooked in big pots.

****

This month I celebrated my 12th year of retirement. Surprisingly it actually has lived up to my expectations. I have not had a single day that I considered boring or disappointing. I am quite pleased with the path I have chosen. My life revolves around family, reading, and gardening.

Seems like something makes me laugh several times every day. Often I laugh at myself. Old folks are funny. We are slow movers. Takes lots of grunting and groaning to get us moving at all. I know in advance that I am going to forget something every single day. I still know my way home. I know what and who is important. I have very few regrets.

Bird's Nest Boots

It's almost 5:30 on Spring Break Saturday morning. I've had my first cup of coffee and sent my husband off to drive a big truck today. When I hear the back door open, it does not surprise me. We are both 70 years old. We forget things. We often make second runs to the bathroom, the medicine cabinet, the coffee pot. This morning

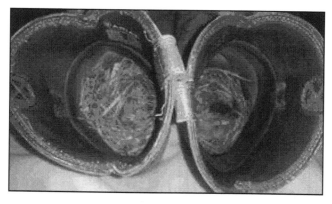

was a definite first. He came back in to show me double barrel bird nests in his old work boots that normally rest on top of our spare refrigerator in the garage. It's Spring! We live in the South.

New Year's Traditions

Lucky Southern menu for New Year's Day meal:

Black eyed peas cooked with hog jowl - luck, luck, luck
Greens - folding money for your pockets
Corn bread - for the basics of life
Tomato sauce - to add a little spice to your life
Pork - because that is what we do

Can anyone add to this? What are you cooking?

****

Not the Best Week

I have not had the best week, But Billy Davis gets in early and takes me down to Jean's on 106. I filled up the back of the car with beautiful flowers and plants. We finished up right before the rain moved in. He just smiled when I teared up. He gets me.

****

Went for routine medical appointment in Montgomery today. The medical assistant remarked that I must have been busy since this time last year. Noted that I wrote down that I had four children now and that I only had two before. Also wore two totally different earrings. We have made it back to Luverne. Maybe I should stay parked for a few days!

Thanks for making my life more meaningful. I wish all older

people would learn to use Facebook. This week I was allowed to welcome babies into several families of friends and relatives. I was able to say Happy Birthday to 8-10 people with whom I had previously last contact. I was able to check on the sick and dying. I congratulated a winner and consoled a loser. I was able to view a marriage proposal, a gender reveal, and a prom invitation. I saw a Father/Daughter school dance. I witnessed a winning homerun. I saw a beauty pageant queen and the winner of a half marathon. I did not have an argument or disagreement with anybody. I shared dozens of laughs, shed a few tears, and had an innocent flirtation with a guy a third my age. Thank you, Mark Zuckerberg.

****

Just a random observation, has anyone else noticed that there are no photos of ugly grandchildren on Facebook? Does that mean there are no longer any unattractive kids or are people hiding them? I know, I know. I might have too much time on my hands, but it needed saying.

The Big 50

At the Vocational Center on Woodford. Ricky Bowers brought me the cake and a hug. We all laughed about how old I was. Enjoyed our early morning coffee and conversation together, as we waited for the buses to roll in with our Brantley and Highland students. Mary Pryor , Sharon Stricklin, Larry Burnett, Jimmy Morgan, Ricky and Yvonne Noble was our chief. We lost Rick in 2006. If I

am wrong about any of the faculty, just correct me. It all becomes a blur now. I spent 20 years at Woodford. Was transfered to Luverne the year the huge renovation was completed. Worked 26 years with the Board of Education and 3 more as a Public Health nurse. Also worked several years as Director of Nursing at the old Nursing Home. Been retired since 2005. About time for a big birthday.

****

Got a demo of the best of man and the worst of man yesterday at Tiger Towne on the way home from Atlanta. Table near us at lunch complained so much that the manager gave them a free meal for the entire group. They did not leave a penny for the sweet, young waitress who had nothing to do with the speed of the kitchen staff. Then we went outside and some nice person had left a note on the driver side door that we had a bolt stuck in a brand new tire. We were saved from a flat on I-85 by a good person! Sort of evened out the day!

****

We came in from a beach trip on a Monday night a few weeks ago. I rushed out to our car to help Billy unload and was running back to catch Maks on Dancing With The Stars and totally busted my butt on the cement slab floor in our garage. I was not hurt at all. I told Billy that I didn't need to bother Blue Cross/Blue Shield with a bone density test because I passed the biggest test. Billy worried about me and then when he realized that I was okay he laughed and said that if it weren't for that silly show that I would not have been running anywhere. He is right.

****

D Other Woman

Billy named his boat. Maybe you remember that the grandchildren call him "D". I am not threatened by a boat, but he does spend more money on her than he does on me. Ha, ha!

****

When you are retired.....you do lots of things you never thought you would have time to do. I keep a daily journal. I grow some flowers just for me and I save quotes from interviews and books. I just looked over my many quotes and came upon this one. It touched me today! Had to share once again.

My granddad said all the time, "Tavis, there are some fights that ain't worth fighting even if you win. There are other fights that you have to fight even if you lose."
Tavis Smiley on Meet The Press – April 17, 2011

****

Billy got up and out before daylight this morning on a day fishing trip to Destin. I feel so much better, but I lolled around all morning watching the Sunday morning news shows. Been stretched out in the sunshine enjoying a new book, listening to the birds chirp. Have cleaned the kitchen, washed a couple of loads of clothes, and paid a few bills. Amazing what I now see as a good day. Billy will bring back some supper that I don't have to cook. I've chatted with both kids. They called me. Everybody is well, for a change. Don't know a single thing I need or want. This old lady is content.

****

Big Chill Soundtrack

I Heard It Through the Grapevine......Marvin Gaye
My Girl................................The Temptations
Good Lovin'....................................The Rascals
The Tracks of My Tears....................Smokey Robinson & the

211

Life is... Later.

Miracles

Joy to the World .... Three Dog Night

Ain't Too Proud to Beg .... The Temptations

(You Make Me Feel)
Like a Natural Woman .... Aretha Franklin

I Second that Emotion .... Smokey Robinson & the
Miracles

A Whiter Shade of Pale .... Prcol Harum

Tell Him .... The Exciters

(I want this played at my memorial.)

****

The big 65! Love the flimsy Medicare card that looks like they only expect us to last a few more months! I plan to disappoint them and hope you do too!

****

Got up at 4:00 this morning.....deliberately. Had a doctor's appointment in Dothan at 7:30.....deliberately. When I am not allowed coffee, I have to get on with it. I rested my eyes most of the way south. Pleased that I noticed this sunrise near Brundidge and made one picture. Rode a few more miles. Billy then told me I was snoring. Bad move! We could ride to Alaska and I could snore the entire way and we still wouldn't be even. He was also sipping coffee from a Yeti mug which means it was still hot and he had such amazing coffee breath that I almost asked him to pull over for a Monday morning French kiss. But then there is that ever present Backwoods Sweet cigar that he holds between his teeth from daylight to dark. He never lights one. I pay that extra money to PEEHIP retired teacher health insurance because I know he has nicotine and tobacco in his blood stream. He is not a smoker, but he costs me. Most days he is worth it, but some days he almost crosses that line.

We made it to the far side of Dothan, on time. I got another neck shot. I got a big IHOP breakfast. I sucked the bottom out of two pots of their fine, hot coffee.

I purchased a few fall plants outside at Home Depot. Billy went in Bed, Bath, and Beyond for Keurig pods, followed by a trade off stop at Gander Mountain for a new rod. He didn't ask what I spent and I didn't ask what he spent. We've been playing these games for nearly 50 years. We both know the rules.

I napped while Billy picked up Will at school. He started the sprinkler when he got home. Life is Good on the Airport Road.

****

During my 26 years of teaching....every single child I taught had special needs! This came to mind as I was reading several posts today!

****

Today was Mama's birthday. She died in 2007. It's been very difficult to get past the dementia and her final nightmare years. Now it's been ten years and some of the good memories have returned.

Mama loved butterflies. I so wanted to plant a butterfly bush in her memory on her birthday. I tried a half dozen nurseries without luck. After the last unsuccessful stop Billy and I made today, I could feel myself start to tear up. So not me. Later in the day, I heard a noise outside. Donny Ray Holmes had dug up one of his very own old time butterfly bushes and planted it in the spot I had picked. There are friends and then there are one of a kind, super special friends. He is the absolute best! Life is Good! Thank you, Donny. Happy Birthday, Mama.

****

My, how the world has changed. I slept a little late and when I rolled over, I heard our television blaring. I heard the excited voices of announcers. Very unusual at my house. We have given up news and begun watching our birds. I thought that maybe there had been another terror attack or another shooting in Washington or another gun in a school. My imagination ran wild! When I opened the bedroom door, I rather frantically asked Billy, "What is it? What's wrong?" He replied, "Since you slept in, thought I'd watch the NASCAR race I had recorded." What a relief! Life is Good! How has this become so routine that we expect bad news? There has to be a better way.

****

Side effects of anesthesia after gall bladder surgery:

I snooze in the car while Julie runs into Publix on Taylor Road. Every time I shut my eyes, there are sideshow creatures surrounding me. If I spot someone walking across the parking lot and shut my eyes, they become monsters. There are monsters coming out of my purse and crawling from under the seat. There is one strange creature that is all flesh and no face. It stretches and strains like a cat in a sack. Thank goodness I didn't get out of the car and run from the monsters.

****

Love a rainy night! Love a rainy Monday morning. Great being retired so I can loll around in pj's , drinking coffee and contemplating life. Good luck to you educators with keeping those sleepy heads awake and involved. Been there. Done that. Homecoming

214

week. No place for slugs. You have my admiration.

* *

I watched football Saturday. I didn't play football. Look at that arm! Even as a nurse, I never realized how easy it is to look like you've been in a bar fight. Lots of wonderful things about getting older. This is not one of them. Please notice my clipboard. Still having fun.

* *

Sylvia Gibson, thanks for squeezing me on the list for Glenwood Festival at the Well camp stew. When you messaged me, I jumped straight in the car so that somebody else didn't claim my 3 quarts. I forgot to bring a cardboard box.

The sign in the community center said No Profanity! It did not mention a dress code or specifically state No Pink Pants. Wayne and a lady helped me get my stew to the car. Figured he might mention my attire. Just wanted you to know in advance. By the way, the stew smells delicious. I got it home without spilling a drop.

Life is... Later.

****

July 2014 - What We Liked

Just watched Emmy Nominations. Affirms how with it we are in our late 60s. Picked nearly all our favorite shows, except Sons of Anarchy! Can't win 'em all!

Breaking Bad (AMC)

Game of Thrones (HBO)

Downton Abbey (PBS)

House of Cards (Netflix)

True Detective (HBO)

****

Ace Atkins is my favorite author. So I read his post this morning and I write him and he writes me back. Due to this picture, I have craved a red velvet cupcake all day. Bottom line - It's on Ace!

When I told Billy I simply had to stop at Super Foods about sundown, he agreed, it was totally Ace's fault.

So Billy asks me to pick him up some peanut butter/honey crackers. I bought the last 4-pack of red velvet cupcakes. I could not find a single pack of the crackers he wanted. I wandered and picked up some bananas, a 5-lb. bag of russet potatoes, and two cherry Cokes. There was a lady at the checkout with a big load of groceries in front of me. I placed my few items at the end of the moving grocery line. I turned and made one more run at locating Billy's crackers. When I came back to my cart, the friendly teenage clerk had rung up my stuff along with the customer's before me in line. Oh, no! I apologized profusely to all involved. She summoned a manager on the PA system. He didn't show. Then she totalled up the groceries for the lady in front of me. I had snatched the 2 Cokes, but everything else was paid for. The clerk said, "You do know that lady just went on and paid for your stuff." I literally shouted, "Oh, you can't do that!" The customer pushed her buggy out to the parking lot and pretended not to hear me. The clerk said,."I'm pretty sure she's not letting you pay." I quickly paid for the 2 Cokes and rushed out to our car. I told Billy to drive to the lower parking lot where the young woman was loading her groceries into her back seat. She smiled when she saw us, but said you're not paying me back. We tried to hand her some cash and she wouldn't take it. I could feel my cheeks flushing. I think I looked so flustered and old that she thought I needed a good deed. She smiled and said, "Someday I might need something." I think this young woman may have been our waitress several years ago at a local restaurant. Billy said I remember her beautiful eyes. Whoever she is and wherever she came from, Thank You. I hope I was nice and tipped her well when I last saw her. I always try to be on the giving end. Receiving from another is a very humbling experience. I won't soon forget this. See what you started, Ace Atkins.

217

Life is... Later.

****

My birds lined up staring into my kitchen window. Apparently sleeping 30 minutes longer than usual has disturbed the delicate balance of nature in my world. Billy says I have trained the birds to avoid foraging for their own breakfast. They depend on me to scatter seeds on the back deck. His theory applies to wildlife, not domesticated spouses.

****

Sometimes a moment is so perfect that you want to bottle it and sleep with the memories under your pillow. Last night was that sort of moment.

Been over 20 years since I had a child performing at an LHS game. Wonderful to watch the kids and grandkids of my friends and former students play ball, cheer, dance, and march with the band. One of those special times when you thank God that you have lived long enough to enjoy the good stuff.

****

This morning as I looked down at my Yeti Ya Ya mug to make sure the spout was in the right position, my neck popped loudly. It startled me and then it popped again and quickly established a rhythm. I was frozen in place and tried to figure what about my pitiful cervical vertebrae could be making this strange, continuous noise. There was a definite bass beat to this. When I reached for my cell phone, right before I speed dialed Dr. Pat, I noticed that my phone screen was showing some rap performance. My volume was set low, but not low enough that I didn't mistake it for a neck noise. Not even a joint issue. This was a simple youtube event. I never had much rhythm, but this morning I was rocking. Life is Good! Elderly life is entertaining! You might as well laugh!

****

Billy went fishing this weekend. Wes was at Lake Martin. Will was with his Mom. Julie and Bill were at a Pennsylvania wedding. I was at home....where I wanted to be, by the way. Occasional solitude is good for the soul. Growing up with three brothers and a house full of friends was fun, but there was not much privacy.

Straight from there to a nursing school dorm with all its estrogen and drama. Then a long, unplanned career teaching teenagers serious skills in the midst of high school bedlam and silliness. I can enjoy a quiet weekend all alone. It helps to have a sweet neighbor who checks on me and pops by to visit. Home with flowers, wildlife, and Netflix is my own special haven. I am very aware of my many Facebook friends who live alone. It has to get old and too quiet. Billy Davis came home earlier than expected bearing gifts.... fresh seafood from Sexton's and Krispy Kremes. Solitude left with a quick hug and a kiss. The best of both worlds.

****

Perfect Mother's Day! Piddled with my flowers while Billy mowed the grass. Billy took me to Jean's Nursery on 106 and I came home smiling. Got tulips, cards and chocolate from the boys. Then Wes grilled for supper. Of course I had several conversations with my daughter and son in law.

****

Happy, Happy Birthday to You! Love you and so love our friend-ship! A priceless friendship is what we enjoy. Last year when I was so upset because I missed grabbing my Moonflower seeds before they sold out, Janice Hall mailed me some. Probably the sweet-est gift I ever received. This is a real picture of one of dozens of blooms! Enjoy your day!

****

I think I have killed my lavender plant. After the fact, I bothered to read up and I think too much water and not enough sun. I clipped the plant back and because the leavings smelled so great....well, I put the stems and leaves in a zip lock bag. Have them right next to my recliner. Get the picture? Ignorance is bliss. No, I am not smoking it!

****

Exciting morning at the Davis household on the Airport Road. The ritual reading of the rain gauge and the answer is......wait for it, wait for it. ....3.1 inches. Amazing what provides entertain-ment for senior citizens. Note that Billy never rounds that number off. He said that if he was being extremely accurate, it read 3.15.

Our rain gauge does not have those intricate measurements, but I have a husband with skills. We got a good rain and are excited about it.

****

If you remember these billboards, you're dating yourself. Now it would be deemed child porn or something inappropriate. My Daddy believed in sun protection before it was a big deal. If I spent the day with a friend and come home sunburned, Daddy considered it bad parenting on the part of the friend's folks. I never learned to worship the sun. Sun bathing was a waste of time to me. I tried it and it took time away that I could have used reading. Daddy was so dark, but none of his kids were naturally brown. My brothers tanned much better than I did. Mama had fluorescent white legs. I think she was anemic most of her life. I took after her in too many ways to name.

I always used sun protection products on my kids. I always wore a long sleeve shirt and started dragging a bedsheet to the beach. When Julie was in Jr Hi, she begged me to sit far away from her in the sand. She didn't want anyone to associate her with the mummy character who was swaddled in the sheet. I figured my job was to embarrass my daughter. At the beach, I managed quite well to be the parent from hell.

The last time I stayed at the coast, I found the beach behavior to be most entertaining. The sheer amount of beach supplies required was astounding. In my day....a beach towel and a set of plastic flip flops met my needs. Now families use huge canvas wagons to roll "essentials" to the water's edge. These folks are better stocked than the settlers moving West in Conestoga wagons. They even have tents. Staking out territory entails getting up early and setting the tent. Usually this takes two husbands with the wives screeching from the condo as to location. This must mean that young men are somehow cut from a different cloth than my beloved of nearly 50 years. Billy Davis does not get up early at the beach. He does not take directions, especially not when shouted.

I can no longer walk in beach sand. Friends ask me, "What do you do at the beach?" Well, I people watch. I remember old family beach trips. I have the best time on a shady balcony. I can do alone for hours. There are no bad days at the beach. After one reaches 70, there are no bad days anywhere.

Happy, Happy Birthday to You! I have such memories of our nursing home days. You were and are such a loyal friend! You never forget the people who tossed you a life preserver when you are in deep water and drowning. Enjoy your special day! Love you always!

****

Can't Help Loving Billy

Billy has gone to help Wes mow schools. As he was leaving, he stopped to brag on my pretty morning glories. He watched the hummingbirds buzz each other for their chance at the feeders. He laughed at the birds lined up to get at the seeds I toss every morning on the deck. How can I not love that man?

****

My maternal grandparents from Birmingham! I am my Grandmother Williams! I am her size, have her age spots, and developed those huge ear lobes that I so wanted as a child. Be careful what you wish for! She was great! Loved sports and only wore a bra on Sundays! Definitely my role model!

****

Weather radar looks spooky. Get it done and cuddle up safely at home. Don't have a jack o lantern, but orange candles work for me. I lit them last night. Billy asked, "Why are the candles lit?" I didn't have a good answer for that one. I just smiled and mumbled. Works really well with old men. Life is Good! Happy Halloween!

****

An observation. Noticed my hummingbirds fighting over flowers and nectar. Is it normal in nature to battle? We all comment that we hate drama and conflict. Do we mean it or do we give it lip service? Sincere questions. To each his own.

Therapy at Monarca's

A year ago and many times since.

All therapy sessions do not happen in professional offices with diplomas and credentials properly framed and displayed. If you

had supper at the Mexican restaurant last night on Highway 331 in Luverne, Alabama, you may have been annoyed by the rowdy, very loud gathering of "retired" educators. If you weren't a local, you would never have suspected that some of this group are in the midst of recent family tragedies, fairly serious illnesses, and dramatic life changing events. Hope any unsuspecting strangers simply saw a table load of silliness. Nothing heals like laughter, hugs, and a Southern drawl.

****

Some critter has come down my chimney and is banging around in the fireplace. It is sealed in by glass doors, but my imagination is just too well developed to allow me to think it is simply a bird flapping its wings. Evacuation is definitely an imminent possibility. Monday morning.....really?

****

Of course, my son solved the mystery of the fireplace monster. Large bird wedged itself between the inner screen and the outer glass doors. Wes even figured out why. It was pursuing an extremely large grasshopper. Bird kept struggling and banging against the glass. Wes used a flat bladed knife and eased the creature to freedom. He is my hero and no snakes involved.

****

Best Southern supper ever. Little white peas. Field corn, picked, shucked, and straight into the pot. Sliced tomatoes with Vidalia onion. That's it.

****

If I got a phone call from the Good Lord giving me a free ticket to Heaven, I would miss out because I would just know he was a telemarketer and would hang up too fast. Don't you wish we really could phone Heaven? I have a couple of questions for Mama Mary. I want to tell Mamaw (Annie Lou Folmar Perdue) that I still think of her every day. Want to tell Daddy Guy that I miss his corny jokes. I want to thank my mother-in-law one more time for the way she raised her boy. Just want to remind my many fabulous aunts and uncles that I still love them. Want to tell my younger first cousin that I hope to see her before long. Just a random thought from this same time last year. Gone, but not forgotten.

****

This is a skink. Actually I think this is a snake with some insignificant, barely there, scrawny legs. This has not been my best gardening year, but I am a heck of a skink farmer. I love little green lizards. They remind me of our trip to The Keys about 10 years ago. I enjoy their company on our deck. Jimmy Buffet music starts wafting from my memory bank when I see one. May I say that lately I very seldom see a green lizard. I suspect that skinks eat lizards. I am positive that skinks are not scared of humans. I just don't trust a critter that won't flinch when you holler "Get!" and come after them with a limp porch broom.

Yesterday Billy was working with Wes on the lawn crew. He sort of made me promise to stay in the house while he was gone. I am recuperating from some dental surgery, but not really incapacitated. I became aware of some tomatoes and some little new potatoes that really needed to leave my kitchen. I put them in a Walmart bag and was just going to ease a half dozen steps to the big garbage can under the carport. I left the back door open and was going to slip back inside the house. If Billy had left the door ajar, I would have fussed. But he doesn't have to know every little thing. As I

closed the lid to the can, a huge skink came charging from behind our outside refrigerator. He scooted between me and the open back door. I've never observed one moving that fast. I was concerned that something was chasing the skink. I was right! A second skink was right behind the first. It was larger and faster and too dang close to the open door. They disappeared under a pot of Swedish Ivy. It remains unknown if the chase involved warfare or romance. I can live without an answer to that question. I hobbled into the house and slammed the back door. I said a little prayer, thanking the Good Lord that these almost snakes did not get inside my house. Then I chuckled because there is always Plan B. Donny Ray Holmes would have come up and removed the skinks and he never would have told my spouse.

I think I have learned a lesson. Sometimes lessons don't stay learned. Also, if you have some green lizards you want to get rid of, I'll trade!

****

Y'all are gonna think I am making this up. Billy was on the porch and got stung by a wasp when he walked by the garbage can. He grabbed the wasp spray and hit everything flying. For good measure, he gave them a thorough cussin'. A couple of hours later, his hand was blown up like the Hulk's. Been to Doc for a shot and taking Benadryl. At the moment the score stands at Critters 3 - Davises 0.

****

This may be my last craft project. Simple silk roses with four glittery hearts for Mama Mary's four children. Pat, Bob, Jim, & Tom. The fact that hot glue oozed out of the trigger handle of the gun onto both my hands does not assure me that Mama appreciated my feeble efforts. I thought my crippled knees meant my dancing days were done. Not so! Sorry no video and especially glad there was no audio.
Love you, Mama. Happy Valentines!

Life is ... Common Ground

FYI It leans to the left, just like Mama. — in Emmaus Cemetery Luverne Alabama.

****

Another one of my stories. We were all at Lake Martin this time last year to celebrate Father's Day and Julie's birthday. Julie is a marvelous hostess, but I cannot stay at her place because my bad knees will not allow me to climb steps to the bedrooms. So Billy and I sleep at the little golfers motel about a block from the house. By little, I mean four rooms. We stay with the kids til bedtime every night. I get up at daylight and must have coffee. I was all set up with coffee, filters, sweeteners, and my half and half cream. The mini refrig was so cold that it froze my cream into a solid milk block. Ever prepared, I packed a can of Pet milk. I found Billy's pocket knife in his inverted cap that he empties his pockets into every night.

I opened the knife and punctured the can. I took the knife back to the bedside table. Couldn't find the magic button to close the blade. Then I stumbled and almost stabbed myself in the chest. In my family, if there is no significant bloodshed, this story is funny. I could hear some people standing outside Turner's whispering, " I guess Billy Davis finally had enough. Hope he gets away with it. He is a good fellow. Bless his heart." I laughed so hard that I woke him up. He closed his knife, rolled over, and started snoring. My coffee was hot and good. I had my cream. We didn't make the Dadeville paper or the Luverne Journal. Just another page in the Billy and Pat marital bliss saga.

227

Life is... Later.

****

Amazing how many dropped pennies appear in my life. Almost any time I am stressed or doubt myself, a penny pops up. I have to believe pennies are a sign. I want to believe. Thank you to my guardian angels.

****

This is yet another one of Pat and Billy's parking spots. The other day we were on the final disk of a good audiobook. We picked up a Subway sandwich and found a pretty local spot to enjoy our lunch and finish our book. Very few cars rode by, but the ones that did saw two old folks sitting in the shade. They got it wrong though. We were two college kids, holding hands, still in love. Have a great day! Life is Good!

****

I am living this show. Never boring here because I am the shining star of my own personal sit-com. Got up before daylight. Made my coffee and heated my hot pack for my stiff neck in the microwave. Loaded all my "stuff" on the seat of my walker. Use it more for transportation purposes than I do for medical reasons. Made it to the bedside. Turned on CNN on my bedroom TV, snagged the hot pack on the walker basket, ripped a sizable hole and scattered the tiny beans and the hot coffee all over the bedroom. I burst out laughing. A clutz does not improve with age. Old folks problems. Life is Good and funny.

****

Woke up early thinking of safety. Lots of posts concerning safety in our schools, safety from terrorism, safety on the highway, safety in our own homes. I was raised by a family that taught safety.... Don't talk to strangers. Look both ways when you cross the street.

Don't play with fire. Don't run with scissors. I heard it so much that I eventually became deaf to it.

Then I fell in love and I felt very protective of someone outside the family. Be careful on the farm equipment, be careful on the highway. God, please don't let him get sent to Vietnam.

Time passed and I married, got pregnant. The script changed. Please be born healthy and perfect. From the moment of birth, I couldn't imagine turning this miracle over to anyone else for protection. And then there were two. Twice the love. Twice the worry.

I was lucky enough to be at home with my babies in the early years. Once I remarked to a group of young mothers at a birthday party that I wouldn't send mine to kindergarten if I didn't have to. There was a sudden silence and I knew I'd be talked about. I didn't care.

There came that first day of school. I rode by the school a half dozen times during that first day and the building didn't burn. There were no deaths on the playground. No kidnappings. I just wanted my child to be safe. My second child later went to daycare and I adjusted.

Time flew by and they survived many activities, field trips, slumber parties, and finally that drivers license. The Mother's mantra that had once been my Mother's became mine. "Be careful! I love you! Call me when you get there."

Suddenly I am a crippled old grandmother, praying for safety for my grandchild and for your kids. I understand every young mother who hugs her child and sends him/her on their way this morning. They want reassurance and guarantees. They seek comfort and answers. I feel your pain, your doubts, and your fears. I hope and pray for an uneventful school day and a special long weekend to cuddle up and cherish family. Please God, let our children be safe.

****

Teaching school prepares one to become a senior citizen. I am presently fairly comfortable saying stupid things and making ridiculous moves. I had lots of practice and there is no better audience to notice your mistakes than teenage students.

Once on the way home from a weekend HOSA competition, our bus lights went completely out. Luckily I was able to pull into the front yard of a house a few miles above Highland Home. As I recall the man of the house came to the door armed with a shotgun. I opened the door of the yellow, minibus that I was driving, nervously stumbled to the doorway and shouted, "Hello! This is a school bus!"

Every student on that bus literally was overcome with fits of loud screams and laughter. Thirty years after the fact, it actually was pretty funny. The nice man put down his gun and invited me into the house to use his phone to call Mr. Joe Rex Sport. We were rescued and I lived to tell this tale.

I expect to hear from some of the "kids" on that bus. What a night!

****

Late yesterday we suddenly noticed an invasive vine had climbed to the top of our tea olive at the corner of the back deck. Somehow Billy and I managed to snatch it down and pile it in the back yard. We inadvertently also removed some of the wild morning glory vines. This morning I walked out at dawn with a cup of coffee in hand. Those morning glories opened one more time. Beautiful and totally amazing. The vine was destroyed, but the blossoms were stunning.

****

All good mothers never stop worrying over their kids. So glad our adult daughter was released from work in mid-town Atlanta and sent home due to the weather. I can relax and enjoy my cold which we apparently shared with our hosts last weekend. Also schools out early and kids headed home soon. Always praying for our school bus drivers and the priceless cargo they haul. Southern folk just don't handle ice and snow very well.

Life is ... Common Ground

****

Now that I have posted family pictures from the beautiful wedding of Mary Cathryn and Chad Brooks, I must confess that as far as Billy and I are concerned.....you can take the rednecks out of the country, but you absolutely cannot take the country out of the rednecks. We enjoyed the weekend in the beautiful Renaissance hotel and the wedding in the swanky Capitol City Club.

I knew something was up when Billy mentioned needing a shoe shine for the third time in about five minutes after we checked into the hotel. I became suspicious and opened his shoe box. Lo and behold his black wingtip dress shoes were crumbling. I believe that if he had walked in them he would have left a trail of black flakes with every step. Dry rot! The shoes literally disintegrated. They were only 20 years old and had not been worn in about 6 months. Only used for weddings and funerals. Hauling chicken litter on an 18 - wheeler does not have a dress code. I should mention that this man has been known to wear boots and shorts. That is a good look for a cute 16 year old female with pretty legs. Sorry I got a tad distracted. Maybe this explains why I simply had to eyeball those wedding shoes.

Our fine son did save the day. When he went to pick up his tux on Saturday morning, he dropped into a shoe store and had his Dad properly outfitted. If I hadn't checked those shoes, we would have beaten the Henagans in our family battle for Crenshaw County Outstanding Redneck Family of the Decade. I just couldn't do that to Mary Cathryn. We came close.

****

I enjoyed the fireworks show from a distance. Took a little glass of wine, a lawn chair and sat in my driveway. There was a pleasant breeze blowing. The smaller fireworks were behind the treeline, but the big ones were above the trees and very pretty. Seemed like the red, white, and blues showed up the best. Life is Good right here in the USA!

Life is... Later.

****

Daddy's sister, Judy Perdue, fell last Sunday night. She went downhill so fast and died on Thursday night, March 3. This has been the most hectic week I think I have had since I retired. Billy and I spent last weekend with Julie and Bill in Atlanta. We stopped in Montgomery on the way home for a routine dermatology visit for Billy. My hand is healing slowly and my pathology report was good and there will be no more cutting. We got home pretty late Monday afternoon. The next three days were spent running back and forth to the Lakehaven Assisted Living where my aunt was a resident. She was clear until the day she died. She made so many cute little jokes that I wanted to share a few. When I commented that I was sorry she had a bad fall, she quickly told me that there are no GOOD falls. Too true. She also commented to Jim that all he could have done for her was be there and catch her when she fell and that it was too late for that now.

The day that she died I rode down to the ALF in my p.j.s to drop off some supplies to some of the staff as they were headed from the parking lot into work. I had turned Will over to Wes at school without getting dressed for the day. I found out that Judy had taken a sudden turn for the worse. I went in wearing some tacky kitty cat socks that she would have approved of and my hair was standing on end. I had on no makeup. When I asked if she needed anything, she said, "You!" I was soooo glad that I went on inside in my state of disarray because later after I went home and got dressed for the day and came back to town....Hospice had sedated her and we never had another conversation.

I think everyone knows that she was the cat lady. There was a big mama cat that spent her last day at Judy's window keeping guard. That night when Turner's came to pick her up that cat supervised the process and watched until the hearse was driven away. Tom and I both had chill bumps. It was amazing.

Friday I read to the second graders at Luverne Elementary and ran a dozen errands helping Daddy get things done at Turner's and in town. Saturday Billy and I had a big day planned in Birmingham. I went to a huge nursing facility to see Mama's brother, James Williams. He is very foggy, but I was glad that I went. Billy and I ate lunch with my Aunt Helen, Mama's sister and we thoroughly

232

enjoyed our time with her. I then went to a baby shower for my nephew's wife. It was sweet and I won a prize for guessing how many inches wide her belly would measure. I think I am way too qualified for that game.....and it has nothing to do with pregnancy. We wrapped up our Birmingham day with dinner with a friend (Vera Wilson) from our Class of '65 and her husband in Alabaster. Whew!!! A packed day and pouring rain from the time we left home until we got back. I had made a pledge to see my relatives at times that do not involve funerals. That is a personal New Year's Resolution worth keeping.

Sunday was my Aunt's funeral in Luverne. Judy tried to make me promise not to do anything when she died. I told her that was too white trash for the Perdues. We had a family conducted short memorial at the cemetery. She was cremated and she already had a small marker at the bottom of Mamaw's slab. Somehow even in the horrible weather, Turner's managed to bury her ashes and have the death date added to the marker. Everything looked perfect. We had a simple pretty flower arrangement and maybe 25-30 people attended. The weather was so raw. All nieces and nephews were present and accounted for. Jim and Tom spoke and did a beautiful job. Bob played Amazing Grace on his harmonica. It was so very sweet. I do think my Aunt Judy would have approved. She always liked cats better than people and somehow I think that she is surrounded by them this morning.

Julia Perdue never married, never had her own children, never knew how pretty she was. I named my first born after her. I am glad I did.

****

So we are wrapping up the month of May. Looking back over my month.....after five end of year school events, five medical appointments, trips to Atlanta and Destin, one dance performance, at least ten nice restaurant meals and oh, yes, book club.....I am tired, but in a happy, grateful way. Wonderful to have a busy life that revolves around family, flowers, and fun! Life is Good!

****

Life is... Later.

This Little Piggy

This is a cautionary tale about joking with gullible children. When I was a little, bitty girl, my grandparents raised pigs on their farm north on Luverne, Alabama. I spent many nights with them. Often a sow would birth in the middle of the night. My granddaddy would go out into the cold and check on his pigs. One night he brought in a tiny piglet. He told Mamaw that the runt would die if he left it in the pig pen. He also said there were so many baby pigs born that the sow didn't have enough "teats" for all her babies.

I couldn't wait to cuddle the baby. I sat by the gas space heater in my flannel nightgown and imagined becoming a pig farmer. After my granddad washed up and came into the kitchen with me, I begged to keep the baby. He told me that he gave the extras to a lady on the road now called Quail Tower. I begged "Just this once".

He said, "We kept a little runt one time and look how that turned out." "Where is it?", I asked. He said, "Look in the mirror." I fell for it. He said I was just too cute to give up. For about a year I walked around believing I was a runt pig born on Perdue Farm in Luverne. I really think the Stork story is more glamorous, but I was stuck with this one. Kids with good imaginations know no boundaries. Oink, oink!

****

Maybe my husband is anticipating the apocalypse and forgot to mention it to me. I checked the expiration date.....2020! We may both expire long before this Spam does. Billy Davis does the majority of our grocery shopping. I must stay prepared for these unexpected purchases. I have never, ever put Spam on a grocery list. We'll discuss this tonight. He's mowing today. My husband, my son, and my grandson are working together until the rain moves in. I am home alone....with the Spam.

****

Had a random, early morning thought. If monogramming had been popular when I was a kid I would have been in for a world of hurt. #1 I grew up in my cousin's hand-me-downs. #2. I was not given a middle name. Always something to be thankful for.

****

"You're not dead yet, are you?" Billy to me before my first sip of coffee. Explanation: We are home. The holidays are done. Having an intimate, old married couple conversation. His props: Phone charger in one hand. Steaming cup of coffee in other hand. Get it? Living the life in 2017. Roll call. Pat and Billy are present and accounted for.

****

Just a little shout out to the many friends who head back to teach second semester. Very different from that Back to School feeling you had in August. Right? I feel ya! Just a little pat on the back. You got this and in the end, you really do make a difference! You count! Life is Good! Thanks!

The Perdue Way

The Perdues took swim classes about the time we were potty trained. I do remember Mama having to clean out the baby pool at the City Pool due to someone not being quite fully potty trained. I will mention no names because Bob will correct me and I don't think he was the guilty party. No swim diapers back in the day!

After swim lessons were completed and we had successfully passed the test, Daddy would take us to the diving board and toss us into the middle of the "deep part" of the pool. I think we all made it to the side and then we seemed to have the confidence to swim on our own. That was pretty much the story of our lives. You get the lessons. You learn the lessons. You succeed!

Daddy was like a teenage brother to me. He played and he was fun. Mama was the disciplinarian. Daddy often popped corn and we were served our portion in little silver cups that all kids received, monogrammed at birth, and ours were adorably dented and aged by Perdue pop corn parties.

Our parents were really good about always managing to serve us whatever they were eating. We often grilled steaks in the back yard. Most all of us liked pink steak and Daddy tried to cook it that way. He didn't like the taste of charcoal lighter fluid. He had us gather up little sticks and he built his base fire. I remember his steaks being delicious and being outside as he cooked being fun.

Once we went on a Sunday afternoon adventure. Daddy took us behind Luverne Coop and we followed the old railroad track path. I remember that the bridge was gone, but Daddy was coordinated enough to hold each of us and jump carefully from one base pole (railroad cross tie) to the next. Nothing to grasp. nothing to balance. He cautioned us to not move once he picked us up. He made the move four times and we all stayed dry. I figure every kid needs to be able to trust their father just that much. Our granddaddy met us at the back of the swamp and had cold water and Coca Cola for the conquering tribe. What fun!

****

Serious question: How do I determine if I am still sick or if I have become extremely lazy? Not sure there is a medical diagnosis involved here. I was retired for approximately 11.5 years before I started spending all my time in pajamas. Clean pajamas, but I have bed hair. Also I really, really need to shave my legs. The only legitimate excuse for the condition of my legs would be confinement in a body cast. That is not the case. If I had fallen, you would have heard the call on scanners when they asked for backup.

Does this sort of thing sneak up on people or what? I fully participated in family events from Halloween through New Year's. Then I caught this cold. It's been downhill ever since. I am a slug. When I wander into the kitchen, it ends up being for chocolate or hot tea or warming my hot packs in the microwave. I haven't cooked since I made our New Year's black eyed peas at Julie's. Really. If we didn't have dozens of quarts of frozen camp stew and take out from the Chicken Shack, we would be deprived.

Hope you and your family are fairing better. Just warning you, my friends, that I am "sorry" and have drifted into enjoying it. Dangerous territory. Life is still Good, but moving at a mighty slow pace. Please don't tell me that the National Championship game is going to perk me up. Not happening.

What I can see in a flash. This afternoon we were riding around eating boiled peanuts and drinking soft drinks on good ice from Red Rock. We rode by a country cemetery. I saw two women walking away from a grave, holding hands. I just saw the backs of their heads. Couldn't tell if the combo was mother/daughter, two sisters, or what. It is Memorial Day weekend. Couldn't help wondering if they were visiting the grave of a fallen soldier.

Grief doesn't pick and choose. It lands on the shoulder at the moment of loss and it's harder to get rid of than a huge tick. We need to think of the sacrifices made so that we have the rights that we enjoy. Fly your flags. Say a little prayer. Whisper "Thank You" before this holiday ends.

****

Life is... Later.

Love is blind! Thank goodness! Bad hair day here, but turn about is fair play. Billy just left to drive a big truck. Picture this: Shorts with work boots. Sweat band. Blue tooth ear piece and an unlit cigar sticking out of the side of his mouth. I love him so much and he did fill the bird bath on his way out. God love him.

****

We got up about daylight and once we got past the big news that Lindsay Lohan was out of jail and then found out who designed Chelsea Clinton's wedding gown...my beloved turned to me and asked, "Do you think there's coffee in Heaven?" We have now covered all the important topics. Have a great day, y'all.

****

Rode out to the cemetery yesterday. Billy straightened Mama's flowers. Rode up the hill and stopped for a moment where I could see my Dad, Granddaddy, great grandfather, and my precious Folmar grandmother and my aunt, Judy Perdue. Will was polite, but unimpressed. One day he will most likely make this same drive-by, hopefully with an innocent child who is unaffected by the experience.

My Mamaw had a favorite saying that I love. "If your family members die in the right order.....You have had a good life." I carry her words in my heart. She shaped me.

****

Somewhere I read that your mother is the one person on earth who is really interested in the trivial details of your life! I miss that about Mama Mary!

****

Life is ... Common Ground

We just finished our latest audiobook. 11 disks. We did a lot of riding and listening. Found this tree on the backside of Emmaus Cemetery in Luverne. Think some woodpecker worked out its frustrations on the trunk. Wondered if it had anything to do with the location. Cemetery visiting is a family tradition. I have many, many relatives who rest there. Folmars are renowned nature lovers. Bet they've been watching that determined bird, listening to his rat-a-tat-tat, chuckling at the damage he's done to a healthy tree. They were porch sitters, wooden swing lovers, rocking chair movers. They did old age very well.

You never know how a life stage is going to fit until you get there. I don't know what it says about me to be so comfortable with being a senior citizen. I can only guess that when you get toward the end of anything, it becomes more dear or not. I don't preach to the young to slow down and savor life's simple pleasures. Not sure that it's possible anyway. Meanwhile we'll keep listening to our books, keep riding around the county, enjoying our golden years.

Life is... Later.

****

Yesterday I went to the Courthouse to get my Handicapped placard for the car. Sorry to need it, but thankful to get it. All the clerks and our Judge Tate were as nice as they could be. I also discovered that I could renew my drivers license a few weeks early. I was told that now you must remove your glasses for the official license photograph.

I did as I was instructed, but when I was given my temporary license.....those people had put a picture of an old, grey headed lady with wrinkles and several chins. I didn't think that was one bit funny. Billy said Forget about it. Let's go eat at the Chicken Shack. Just giving you a warning. Those people love pranks.

****

My job is to get an American flag out for any and all flag flying holidays. I try to make sure Mama's is slightly larger than the male veterans in her area. If you don't get this...... well you just didn't know our Mother all that well. God Bless America.

****

Facebook test: Choices

1 Hair down or up? No choice.
2 Jeans or yogas? yogas
3 Painted or non painted nails? toes, yes. fingers, no
4 Favorite color? blue
5 t shirt or dress shirt? XXL t shirt
6 flip flops or sneakers? flip flops
7 Big purse or small? Big granny purse
8 Tattoos? In my dreams
9 Piercings? NO. Even virgin ear lobes
10 Diamonds or pearls? wedding set and none since
11 Favorite animal? puppies that belong to someone else
12 Favorite food? sushi
13 Rap or country music? neither

14 Height? 5'7" prior to osteoporosis
15 Sports or Couch? SEC football on big flat screen from the couch

****

I have been saving my fortunes from the cookies at Chinese restaurants for the past few years! These are some of my favorites.

You have a keen sense of humor and love a good time.

You will have good luck and overcome many hardships.

You need not worry about your future.

Good health will be yours for a long time.

And my number one favorite and working so well for me:
You are going to have a very comfortable old age!

****

I bought a pack of little white peas at Super Foods. I felt guilty due to the price and started thinking about my granddaddy, Virgil G. Perdue. He always had a beautiful vegetable garden. It was weed free. I don't know how he managed that, but he was meticulous. He had a garden water pump and always had to carry a bucket of well water to prime the pump. I asked him to explain why he had to carry water to a water pump. He was not a patient man, but Duzzer took time to explain the process to a curious child. He ended his explanation with this statement, "This is one of those times if you don't put something in, you won't get anything out." This has stuck with me for more than 60 years. I think it applies to relationships, employment situations, and life in general. Children learn many important lessons that have nothing to do with school and classrooms. I was blessed then and am blessed now.

I am including this picture that reminds me so much of my grandmother. I remember what we talked about while Mamaw shelled peas and snapped beans from Duzzer's garden. Good times.

****

Life is... Later.

Once a Perdue, always a Perdue. Gotta love this. Sent my husband to pick up our camp stew order. Can't locate what I ordered. We have only been married 46 years. Only in a small Southern town are women forever known by our maiden names. Personally, I wouldn't want it any other way. To make my day even better, I had to go to the car to get my I.D. to buy a bottle of peach wine at Dollar General. 68 and still getting carded. Life is Good and funny!

****

Friday afternoon I was at a boat ramp in Ft. Walton. There was a nice looking guy in his late thirties who had played on a jet ski until he was totally exhausted. He finally loaded his jet ski on a trailer and was leaning against a pick-up truck waiting to get his breath back and for his legs to stop feeling like wet noodles. This is the statement that I overheard:

"God, I wish I was 15 AND had some money AND some sense." I think that pretty well sums it up in a nutshell.

****

Saturday afternoon about dusk I was at a different boat ramp. The spot was suddenly overrun with giant cranes. Seagulls look okay to me and I sort of like the sweet calls they make. Cranes, if they were dogs, would be stray, mangy mutts. These were all about three feet tall when they landed. There were probably 20 or more that congregated at the end of the boat ramps. I soon noticed that there were two women who obviously feed these cranes often. The birds recognized the car that the women drove and parked at the end of the boat ramp....very much in the way of the boats and trucks that were using the ramps. Due to the sudden onslaught of cranes, the whole scene resembled something out of that Hitchcock movie. Not one of my personal favorites. Now when a crane poops the volume of excrement closely equals the consistency and volume of a small Wendy's Frosty. Sorry to ruin that for any of you fans. The birds and the women took over the boat ramps. These strange women had named the individual birds....who honestly all looked the same except for one that had a crippled leg.

I pretty well knew what was coming next. Some little child had the audacity to run at the cranes and was chewed out by the crane women. This child appeared to be in the company of a grandmother was raised much better than I was. She did not bark back at the women and took her grandchild by the hand and walked away.

Not so lucky with next encounter. A nice boat pulled up to the ramp. I noticed a teenage boy who slipped a little in the bird poop and shooed the cranes away. One of the women started to reprimand this young man. He was in the company of a pretty young woman who was incidentally worthy of the bikini she was wearing. The boy's parents had been on the boat ride. When one of the crane women commented rather loudly, "I thought only children acted like that!" The teenage boy blushed and said, "Lady, it is a f***ing bird!" In all my life I have never gone along with the use of that word until yesterday. The parents immediately corrected their son and as they walked past me apologized. I told them that I had been watching these women and that they were "nuts'. The boy came over, shook my hand, and personally apologized to me and said that he loved animals. I told him that I had taught teenagers for years and that he had not scarred me for

Life is... Later.

life. I told the family that these women were hunting trouble and that there was plenty of deserted space right down the water's edge that would have been far away from people and the boat ramps. I have matured to the point that I did not walk out on the ramp and clap my hands and frighten the birds. In my 40s, I probably would have done just that. Always something to see at a boat ramp.

****

On Friday night, Billy and I took a sunset boat ride. I enjoyed it and we were right in area of a small shopping center when we trailered the boat. I first went to the liquor store. My children had recently introduced me to some little individual bags that contain ready to drink margaritas and peach daiquiris. Store them in the freezer and they are ready to drink the minute you pull them out. Not really a good idea, but they sell those things everywhere. You might need an ID to purchase them....none before 21 and maybe none allowed after 55, but too late now.

I next went to Publix and bought some supplies for the weekend. I thought we were all set and ready to go in for the night until I saw the HOT sign shining brightly at the Krispy Kreme donut shop. We were towing a boat and Billy told me that there was no way to stop in the parking lot. I talked him into pulling into the lot next door. I climbed through shrubbery in the dark and knocked a few homeless people out of the way as I made my way to the hot doughnuts. My husband has enjoyed this story so much because I am rather unsure on my feet until I spot that special sign and then I am just fine. We all have our priorities.

We had a marvelous weekend and there are always stories to tell. Bear with me on my ramblings and remember....there is a special delete button on every computer.

****

I'll Confess My ABCs

A- Age: 68

B- Biggest Fear: dementia
C- Current Time: 11:15 am on Sat., August 8, 2015 CST (daylight savings)
D- Drink you last had: coffee
E- Easiest Person To Talk to: my daughter on commute chats
F- Favorite Song: Still the One
G- Grossest Memory: Perdue boys' old tennis shoe aroma
H- Hometown: Luverne
I- In love with : Billy Davis for nearly 50 years
J- Jealous Of: women with a wad of grandkids
K- Killed Someone? only with kindness
L- Longest Relationship: Bob, Jim, and Tom, my bros
M- Middle Name: not one
N- Number of Siblings: three
O- One Wish: For family to die in the right order.
P- Person who you last called: Kay, sister-in-law
Q- Question you're always asked: Did you know Mary Perdue?
R- Reason to smile Will Davis, always
S- Song you last sang: The Big Chill soundtrack
T- Time you woke up: 5:30 a.m.
U- Underwear Color: who cares?
V- Vacation Destination: Destin
W- Worst Habit: forgetting names
X- Xrays you've had : Full body
Y- Your favorite food: Sushi (tuna)
Z- Zodiac Sign: Pisces

****

My grandmother taught me how to be old. She was a happy person. Mamaw used to chuckle for no apparent reason. She literally whistled while she worked. In her 80s, she still had crushes. She could flirt like a silly teenager. She loved nature and taught me to pay attention to the little things, like snake tracks in sand and a feather caught in a dewy spider web. Getting up early on a cold morning allows me time for recall and reflection. I like to hold a cup of fragrant, hot coffee in my old lady hands. A warm mug is therapy for my creaky fingers. The aroma of creamed coffee can bring back sweet memories of a warm country kitchen and unconditional love. Those memories must have been tucked in some cozy corner and now I can seek them, but only in a comfortably silent moment. Young women don't get much silence. Working women don't find much down time. Old women, if they choose to, can experience their own special time travel. It's truly like Mamaw left me special gifts, but I've only just gotten around to opening them. Thank you, Mamaw! Life is Good! I'll meet you tomorrow when it's quiet and early.

****

Memories of Mama Mary

Mama is in her room at Lakehaven and she looks nice in a blue velour sweat suit. Maretta has her hair and nails looking so nice. I am impressed. Maretta says that she has never done white hair before, but I tell her that she has done fine with it.

Mama gives me a gift by responding and thanking me. I tell her that she has lots of people who love her. She says that I am good with the loving stuff and she thanks me again. She comes close to making sense. After I leave I almost feel the need to stop the van and cry. I make myself get over it.

Never could have survived those years without Maretta, Judy, Nancy, and the many wonderful people at Lakehaven Assisted Living Facility. They became family and more.

****

Beautiful MLK Day! Hope my teacher friends are cuddled up and sleeping in. I told you last week that a rat had joined my fine feathered friends on the deck. I have another tale to share.... imagine.

Jama Walker wrote a cute tale about her attempt to return a repeat order from Walmart during Christmas. She definitely did the right thing, properly and promptly. Naturally it made me think of a story of my own.

Years ago I had a nice meal with a group of ladies at Capt. Dave's

Life is ... Common Ground

Seafood Restaurant in Destin. The place was packed. Service was slow, but the food was outstanding. Once we finally got our bills and presented our credit cards, it took another 15-20 minutes to settle up. As I was waiting for some of my friends to visit the restroom, I glanced at my bill and noticed that our waitress had not included my bowl of gumbo. Now I was billed for grilled scallops and an adult drink. I was tired, sleepy, and the place was crowded. I didn't go back to hunt down the waitress and correct the mistake as I should have. Right then I made a pledge that I would come back and make it good the next time I was at the coast. I told myself that this was fine and I put it on this whole incident on the back burner.

Within a month there was a big storm and the beachfront restaurant was heavily damaged. Guess you get the picture. There was no way to correct the mistake. I had the scenario play in my mind that I might make it to the Golden Gates and hear that booming voice shout, "Remember that gumbo!" I thought about it more and more often. It was gnawing at me.

Finally Capt Dave's reopened. Billy and I went to Destin. I told him we are going to eat at Capt. Dave's that very night and I was picking up the tab. When we arrived, we were given a nice table with a beach view. I told our waiter to write up two bowls of gumbo, but to only bring one to our table. He looked at me strangely and said "Ma'am?" I explained that I had owed them for a bowl of gumbo and I had come to make it right. He shook his head, but did as I asked. I enjoy the delicious seafood gumbo, but I really enjoyed straightening out this wrong.

The moral of my story is don't take second chances for granted. At least I know I won't be stopped at the Golden Gates due to gumbo. Be assured that there are other personal transgressions to ponder, but this story is long enough for one morning.

****

I am grateful for the sounds my husband makes when he comes home for the night. Love the sound of his pickup door when he slams it. I hear his grunts and groans when he sits on his red stool at the back door and removes his work shoes and puts on his bedroom shoes. Sweetest sound is his key in the back door and his shout "Tricia!" I never, ever take it for granted. Life is Good!

Life is... Later.

Life has dozens of phases. You know like the Terrible Twos, The Horrible Teens, The Empty Nest. I have apparently hit the Clumsy Crest.

Last night, Billy went to sleep while we were watching Netflix. Being the considerate spouse that I am, I attempted to exit the living room and go to bed without disturbing him. I always take my purse to the bedroom for the night. It's an old lady thing. My Birmingham grandmother and my Mother did this. When I picked up my purse, the corner struck a glass of Coke and ice. I soaked every remote controller on the table that sits between our recliners. The table has separate tiles, so the liquid seeped into a little basket underneath that holds the assorted remotes that are not routinely used. Then it seeped to the floor and made a puddle. It takes special skill to make such a big mess with an ounce of watered down soft drink and random melty ice cubes. I confess that the situation required profanity. I don't cuss often, but when I do, I do a thorough job of it. Either I didn't wake up Billy or he pretended to be sleeping so that he didn't have to assist in the clean up. It's almost funny this morning and the good news is that most of the remotes appear to be in working order. It's easy for me to laugh at myself.

Common Ground. So often finding your common ground is not a literal location. With me, this football season, the bottom bleachers in the north east corner of the Samuel Carr, Luverne High School gymnasium is my spot. Somehow, through the grace of God, I have made nearly all the Pep Rallies. In this area, I am not a former grad. I am not a retired teacher. I am not the parent of a former cheerleader and a loud tuba player. I am an old lady with a bright blue cane, a padded cushion, and a true determination not to give it up.....yet.

248

Life is ... Common Ground

I am sitting with other dedicated grandparents. My favorite moments are when the grandkids....the LHS Tigers, the cheerleaders, the band members, the dancers, the flag girls, the senior class members....enter the gym and spot their grandparents in our special spot. Pure love at its finest! I know what's going on in these local families - sickness, financial issues, divorce, tragedy, even death. I love the smiles, the winks, the thrown kisses, and the hugs from these young people presented to their grandparents and other older relatives. Respect is a special gift from one generation to another. It is earned, not given. I embrace my age. Yes, you can measure love! Thank God for this gift of time.

****

I promised to reveal our location yesterday. Billy had an appointment in Destin. We always need a Walmart run. It was a cold, windy day at the coast. The sun was bright. Billy ran errands and I got a long time to observe the people of Walmart from our toasty warm vehicle. As I told you yesterday, the shopper profile was very different in Destin.....no pajama pants, bedroom shoes, or pink rollers in the hair. There are always stories though.

Story #1 I watched an dignified white-haired lady exit the building with a young male Walmart employee pushing her full cart. Immediately I could tell that she was hunting her vehicle. The two would head in one direction and then turn and go in another. The lady was cold, flustered, and feeling stupid. I know because I have been there. The young employee remained calm and patient. Finally they stopped near me and she dug into her handbag. The young man leaned over her and repeated instructions several times. Then I heard the alarm on a distant car begin to blare. The old lady breathed a sigh of relief and the pair moved off in the correct path. I'm sure the scenario was a near nothing to the young man, but I know to the lady he was a knight in shining armor. What a sweet gift of caring respect he gave her! And it cost him nothing.

Story #2 An older gentleman parked right in front of me. He opened the back door of his car and retrieved a cane. He carefully locked the car and walked toward the Walmart entrance. In less than a minute he returned to his car. He opened the back door and swapped that cane for another cane. He locked the car and went inside Walmart. In less than five minutes, the man came back to his car, completely empty handed. He put the cane in the back seat, and drove away. I had a hundred unanswered questions. Bless his heart!

Story #3 There were many parents who brought their kids with them to Destin Walmart on Thursday morning. I did my own personal psychology study while I waited in the sunshine. Nearly every adult female held the hands of the children in their care. Almost all the adult males did not. There were no close calls or truly dangerous situations. My question: Are the females overly protective or are the males building independence? I tend to be a hand holder. Also for all the occasions when my kids snatched their hands from mine, I'm now somewhat prone to snatch my hands from theirs as they attempt to help their old, crippled mother up and down the curb. This behavior has probably existed since cave men occupied our planet. Is there a right way?

See what happens when I'm left alone in a parked car. Have a good Friday and a wonderful weekend! Life is Good for the easily entertained!

****

Affirming Life at Walmart. Yesterday we drove to Troy after visiting our new great niece out in the country. We ate lunch and then Billy planned to drop me at Walmart. I asked him to ride for a few minutes longer. I was out of steam and felt a little bit down in the dumps. After some conversation and some hand holding, I thought I could manage a trip into the store.

When Billy made the stop at the front of Walmart, my bad knee was acting up and I just wasn't sure I could make it to the line of carts inside the store. A good sturdy cart/buggy serves as a walker for some of us wobbly, golden girls. I almost turned around and gave it up when two black women and a little boy walked past me. One of the women shouted, "Miss Pat". She grabbed me and hugged me. It was one of those big, real hugs. I couldn't call her name, but she was one of my former students. Then unexpectedly that precious little boy gently hugged me. He was about as tall as my sorry, worn out knees. He just wrapped his arms around me.

This woman then said "Let me help you." She gave me her arm and when we got to the line of the carts, she pulled one out and got it set for me.

Two Walmart employees were standing near the front and she explained, "This is my teacher from years ago." We had a little chat. She told me to be careful. She said it sure was good to see me and gave me one more hug for good measure and off she went. This little scenario reminded me why I taught and why I stuck with it for over 26 years. My spirits were lifted and those hugs were good medicine for the soul. Seemed like I suddenly felt a little bit stronger and more hopeful. Sometimes the little things are exactly what we need. Once again.....Life is Good!

****

Our old movie theater is getting a facelift. I spotted this from the post office yesterday. Some great memories from what is now Luverne Hardware. I saw Old Yeller there when I was 10 years old. I cried so hard that I had to wait until the crowd left before I ventured out into the sunshine. I can still smell the popcorn.

Life is... Later.

****

There was only one thing about our fantasy family Thanksgiving trip that was not absolutely perfect. Well, actually 8 things. Our vacation bedroom had eight mirrored doors on the closets. These mirrors were on my side of the king size bed. This means every single time I sat on the side of the bed, I was blessed with a panoramic view of my nearly nude 70 year old, heavily padded, well used body. Remember my medical chart story with the harsh description of "elderly, obese white female". For a week, there was no way to ignore the truth. I am so blessed that I have family and friends who love me...... no matter. When I think back about my happy times with both of my grandmothers, I really don't recall how they looked. I loved them so big, they had no flaws. Maybe the memories that remain when I am gone will be kind. I am thankful that we do not have mirror walls in our bedroom at home. Life is Good and love is blind!

I am thankful for any part of my 70 year old body that's still working. I do not mean functioning at a superior level, I mean working at all. You remember having an ancient vehicle as a teenager that would struggle to crank? Remember that noise it made while you prayed for it to get you to class just one more time, to get you home for Christmas, to get you to the dorm parking lot on a freezing night before curfew? That's where my body and I are right now! I'm grateful for every single day! You won't find me complaining about wrinkles, gray hair, and appearances. I'm here! Life is Good!

****

I've mentioned that I have been waking up early and sitting in our darkened living room allowing memories to flow freely. A few days ago I must have drifted off to sleep. Mama was suddenly standing in front of me. She was writing on a big chalk board. Mama used to leave our chore list on a chalk board when we lived in the Bricken house on East First Street. I focused on what she was writing. I realized that it could be very important. She kept looking over her shoulder to make certain I was paying attention. There was a big problem. Her written words were not in English.

252

They looked like Chinese or some language that did not contain our alphabet. The symbols were strange to me. I moved and tried to adjust my eyes. In a puff of mist, Mama was gone. I woke up and was fully alert. Whatever she was trying to tell me was lost. There's probably a Heavenly rule that communication with the Earth bound is prohibited. That would not have slowed Mama up. She was not a rule follower. Since then I have found lucky pennies from Heaven. I have spotted cardinals in my yard. They looked straight at me as they perched on the deck railings. I'll trudge on until I get another message. I'll keep looking and listening for Mama. I am open to suggestion.

****

The really good stuff about marriage is the little stuff. Billy and I had the best time watching movies together. We managed to stay wide-awake and with it. That is quite rare these days and I am usually the guilty party because I love sleep and my bed. That is what seems most old about me now. Well, that and the deep wrinkles above my eyes.
At times Billy's snoring just bugs the fire out of me and at other times I don't even hear him. This was a good weekend and I was so glad to have him home that I slept wonderfully. I dread the widow days and maybe I will miss them. Who ever knows in this old life.

****

DEEP THOUGHTS - HEAVY LIFTING

Support. Heavy Lifting is what the war experts call it about the U.S. being in Iraq in mass. That's what I am into at present. Mama in the midst of her fog depends on me to support her and I support the staff at the Assisted Living Facility. It doesn't amount to all that much in time and effort, but it sucks the joy out of a day like a giant tick. I dread going down to the ALF, which is appropriately situated on a dead end street. The outside is difficult to negotiate and so is the inside. Mama is not Mama any more. She is a thin, wasted shell. She is so sweet and affectionate now. What little speech she can squeeze out is filled with compliments. My hair looks good, my clothes are pretty, even my legs are brown, which they are not, by the way. I guess all the sweet words were hung up somewhere deep inside and I get them now when I am nearly sixty and not when I was an insecure teen. She was never satisfied with my clothes and my hair and my choices. What does it all matter now? Not a bit, but I am still receiving my due that is overdue.

I support Martha in her time of bereavement. I don't support her like anyone else or in the way that others hug and say that they love her and talk in whispery consolatory tones. It is not in me and didn't I just say that it wasn't in Mama when she was younger. Martha told me that I had literally saved her life by spending many weeknights with her while Billy has been gone on the truck. I don't think I am doing much, but I am doing what I can. We eat, boy, do we eat! We watch television while we loll on the leather couches surrounded by wounded animals and grief. And we laugh because we always have. We can't watch the news because the Middle East is too depressing and hopeless, so we watch trivial goulash and we wait for the ten o'clock news that signals we can go to bed in a short while. Martha doesn't turn on her new security system when I am with her. She thinks that maybe I could fight off boogers, which I would probably only sleep through. I get up at dawn and head home to my coffee and my other support job.

I support Wes in the most important way possible. I am providing Will's daily, consistent care. I am being Ya-Ya everyday in the same place at the same time. My time is running out because this time next year he will be enrolled in K4 and won't need me anymore. Wes says daily That he couldn't do it without me. That feels like a heavy weight on my head, but it is not something I planned or anticipated. I just was there and willing. I am filling a role that Mama and Honey ran from. Julie was difficult, but probably not anymore difficult than Will. They did not want to be tied down when they were younger. Mama and Honey were in their late forties and maybe that is the difference. Maybe they knew that I would do an excellent job with Julie. Children don't just happen. So I support and of all my unpaid positions, I like this one the best. I know Will loves me but he doesn't cuddle and show it. I just wait until he says that something is "Me, Ya-Ya." Which clearly means that the two of us are going to do it together.

Am I supporting Billy? Only he can answer that. I know that he loves me and still likes me most of the time. I am doing what he expects me to do. Be there for others. Be less selfish than others. Family isn't the most important thing, it is the only thing.

Life is... Good!

Up early enjoying sunrise, basking in a quiet, warm house, contemplating life. 2018 is a big year for me. Celebrating 50 years out of Nursing School. 50 years of marriage. 50 years since starting my first real job. All my life I've listened to old people talk about how fast life goes by. Now I get it! You blink and suddenly find yourself on the down hill slope. I've always been a rose smeller, a live in the moment person, a cherish the good stuff gal, but regardless.....it all slip slides by anyway. If you spot me driving through town with a smile on my face, now you'll know why. It's because Life is Good and I've got lots of celebrating to do!

81625295R00143

Made in the USA
Lexington, KY
18 February 2018